THE ART OF SOCIAL MEDIA

By now it's clear that whether you're promoting a business, a product or yourself, social media is near the top of what determines your success or failure. And there are countless pundits, authors and consultants eager to advise you. But there's no one quite like Guy Kawasaki, the legendary former chief evangelist for Apple and one of the pioneers of business blogging, tweeting, Facebooking, Tumblring and much, much more. Now Guy has teamed up with his Canva colleague Peg Fitzpatrick to offer *The Art of Social Media* – the one essential guide you need to get the most bang for your time, effort and money.

With over one hundred practical tips, tricks and insights, Guy and Peg present a bottom-up strategy to produce a focused, thorough and compelling presence on the most popular social-media platforms. They guide you through the steps of building your foundation, amassing your digital assets, going to market, optimizing your profile, attracting more followers and effectively integrating social media and blogging.

For beginners overwhelmed by too many choices as well as seasoned professionals eager to improve their game, *The Art of Social Media* is full of tactics that have been proven to work in the real world. Or as Guy puts

ALSO BY GUY KAWASAKI

APE: Author, Publisher, Entrepreneur

Enchantment

What the Plus!

The Macintosh Way

Reality Check

How to Drive Your Competition Crazy

Rules for Revolutionaries

Selling the Dream

Hindsights

The Computer Curmudgeon

Database 101

THE ART OF SOCIAL MEDIA

POWER TIPS FOR POWER USERS

GUY KAWASAKI

and Peg Fitzpatrick

PORTFOLIO
PENGUIN

PORTFOLIO PENGUIN

UK | USA | Canada | Ireland | Australia
India | New Zealand | South Africa

Penguin Books is part of the Penguin Random House group of companies
whose addresses can be found at global.penguinrandomhouse.com.

First published in the United States of America by Portfolio/Penguin,
a member of Penguin Group (USA) LLC, 2014
Published in Great Britain by Portfolio Penguin 2014
006

Illustration credits:
Pages 9, 11, 13, 35, 111, 112, 116, 117, 142, 143, 144, 145,
   146, 147, 176, 177: Google Inc., used with permission
84: MyCrazyGoodLife.Com
96: Peter Adams
97: Photo by Guy Kawasaki
108: Photo by Peg Fitzpatrick
119: Eric Harvey Brown
155: Calvin Lee, Mayhem Studios
169: Photo by Nohemi Kawasaki
Other images courtesy of the authors

Printed and bound in Great Britain by Clays Ltd, Elcograf S.p.A.

A CIP catalogue record for this book is available from the British Library

ISBN: 978-0-241-19947-3

www.greenpenguin.co.uk

Penguin Random House is committed to a
sustainable future for our business, our readers
and our planet. This book is made from Forest
Stewardship Council® certified paper.

ABOUT THE AUTHORS

*There is nothing to writing. All you do is sit down
at a typewriter and bleed.*

ERNEST HEMINGWAY

GUY KAWASAKI is the chief evangelist of Canva, an online design service, and an executive fellow of the Haas School of Business (University of California Berkeley). Previously, he was the chief evangelist of Apple and special adviser to the CEO of the Motorola business unit of Google.

PEG FITZPATRICK is a social-media strategist and director of digital media for Kreussler Inc. She's spearheaded successful social-media campaigns for Motorola, Google, Audi, Canva, and Virgin. When she dies and meets Saint Peter, the first thing he'll say is, "I follow you on Pinterest."

GUY AND PEG are the social-media equivalent of <u>Jack Bauer</u> and <u>Chloe O'Brian</u> in Guy's favorite TV show, <u>24</u>. Guy is Jack: kicking ass and doing whatever it takes with no regard for policies, protocols, and procedures. Peg is Chloe: Jack's trusted friend, on a computer telling Jack where to go and what to do in order to keep the train on the tracks.

CONTENTS

The quality of any advice anybody has to offer has to be
judged against the quality of life they actually lead.

DOUGLAS ADAMS, *THE ULTIMATE HITCHHIKER'S GUIDE:*
FIVE COMPLETE NOVELS AND ONE STORY

READ THIS FIRST

Do not follow where the path may lead. Go instead
where there is no path and leave a trail.

RALPH WALDO EMERSON

The purpose of this book is to enable you to rock social media. We assume that you are familiar with the basics and that you want to use social media for business, either for yourself or for an organization.

To make our perspective clear, Peg and I are in the trenches of social media, not in a "war room" back at headquarters. We acquired our knowledge through experimentation and diligence, not pontification, sophistry, and conference attendance.

Still, do not take our word as gospel. These are our tips, tricks, and insights, and we hope they work for you. In a perfect world, however, you would develop better techniques than ours, and you'd tell us how to improve our game too.

There are two versions of this book: electronic and printed. The electronic version has several hundred hyperlinks (underlined in the print version) that you can click on for added convenience. The printed version obviously doesn't have hyperlinks, but you'll have no problem using it without them.

Finally, let me explain the "voice" of this book. It combines our knowledge, but just one of us, Guy, wrote it, because multiple voices are tiresome for readers and we are all about making everything invigorating, fast, and easy.

Guy Kawasaki
Peg Fitzpatrick
July 2014

ACKNOWLEDGMENTS

If the only prayer you said was thank you,
that would be enough.

MEISTER ECKHART

Thanks to all our beta testers, who made hundreds of improvements to this book: Jessica Ann, Katie Boertman, Dave Bullis, Will Carpenter, Noelle Chun, Katie Clark, Brock Cline, Chris Coffee, Julie Deneen, Mandy Edwards, Sandy Fischler, Héctor García, Isabella Gong, Ian Gotts, Liz Green, Andy Jones, Susan Jones, Stephanie Kong, Stephen Levine, Rachelle Mandik, Dr. Christina McCale, Henry McCormack, Carol Meyers, Lessie Mitch, Heme Mohan, Donna Moritz, Martha Muzychka, Anne O'Connell, Ken Olan, Arya Patnik, Paul Radich, Rebekah Radice, Jerad Reimers, Phillipe Rodriquez, Bernd Rubel, Bonnie Sainsbury, Antonella Santoro, Martin Shervington, Emily Taylor, Jennifer Thome, Thomas Tonkin, Halley Suitt Tucker,

Sarah Wagoner, Stephanie Weaver, Shawn Welch, Erika White, Susan Wright-Boucher, and Joyce Yee.

And thanks to all the people who work for social-media platforms and for the companies that make social-media tools. We could not do what we do without you.

How to Optimize Your Profile

Do what you can, with what you have, where you are.

THEODORE ROOSEVELT

Let's start with the basics. All social-media platforms provide a "profile" page for you to explain who you are. This is for biographical information and images. An effective profile is vital because people use it to make a snap judgment about your account.

The goal of a profile is to convince people to pay attention to your social-media activities. Essentially, it is a résumé for the entire world to see and judge. This chapter explains how to optimize your profile to maximize its effectiveness.

1. Pick a Neutral Screen Name

Before we work on your profile, let's pick a good screen name. Today's clever name, such as @MartiniMom or @HatTrick-Hank, is tomorrow's regret, and you're not going to work for the same company forever, so @GuyMacEvangelist is risky too. Imagine it's two years from now and you're looking for a job. Now pick a name.

You probably already have a screen name, but the longer you use a lousy one, the harder it will be to change it later, and the more negative effects it will cause. Our recommendation is that you use a simple and logical screen name. In my case, that's "Guy Kawasaki," not "G. Kawasaki," "GT Kawasaki," or "G. T. Kawasaki." This is not the place for cleverness or complexity, so make it easy for people to find and remember you.

2. Optimize for Five Seconds

People do not *study* profiles. They spend a few seconds looking and make a snap decision. If this were online dating, think <u>Tinder</u> (swipe right for yes, swipe left for no) versus <u>eHarmony</u> (complete the Relationship Questionnaire).

Your profile should give the impression that you are likable, trustworthy, and competent. Platforms provide space for this information:

- **Avatar.** This is a small circular or square picture of you or your logo.

- **"Cover" (Google+, Facebook, and LinkedIn) or "header" (Twitter).** This picture is the largest graphic element in a profile and visually tells your story.

- **Biographical text.** This is a summary of your education and work experience.

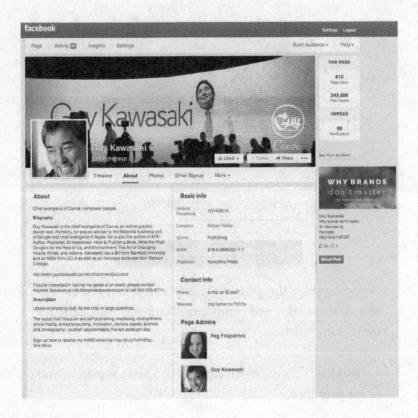

- **Links.** This is a list of links to your blog, website, and other social-media accounts.

3. Focus Your Avatar on Your Face

A good avatar does two things. First, it validates who you are by providing a picture, so people can see which Guy

Kawasaki you are. (God help us if there is more than one.) Second, it supports the narrative that you're likable, trustworthy, and competent.

Your face provides the most data about what kind of person you are. Thus your avatar shouldn't show your family, friends, dog, or car, because there isn't room. This also means you should not use a logo or graphic design unless the avatar is for an organization.

Here are three additional avatar tips:

- **Go asymmetrical.** Symmetry makes a picture less interesting, so don't stick your face exactly in the middle. Divide a picture into thirds and place your eyes near one of the vertical lines.

- **Face the light.** The source of light should come from in front of you. If the light comes from behind you, your face will probably be underexposed unless you force a fill flash on your camera or use a photo editor.

- **Think big.** When people scan posts and comments, they see your avatar at a postage-stamp size. When they click on it, however, they should see a big, crisp photo, so upload a picture that is at least 600 pixels wide.

4. Stick with One Picture

If companies used different logos in different places, mass confusion would reign. Your picture is your social-media logo, so use the same one everywhere. This will help people recognize you on social-media platforms and reduce questions about whether, for example, @GuyKawasaki on Twitter is +GuyKawasaki on Google+.

5. Craft a Mantra

Most platforms enable you to add a tagline to your profile. Make this a mantra—two to four words that explain why you or your organization exists. For example, my mantra is "I empower people." Here are four theoretical mantras for companies:

- **Nike**: authentic athletic performance
- **FedEx**: peace of mind
- **Google**: democratizing information
- **Canva**: democratizing design

Finally, for the sake of consistency, ensure that your tagline/mantra is the same on every service.

About

Chief evangelist of Canva. I empower people.

Biography

Guy Kawasaki is the chief evangelist of Canva, an online graphic design tool. Formerly, he was an advisor to the Motorola business unit of Google and chief evangelist of Apple. He is also the author of APE: Author, Publisher, Entrepreneur--How to Publish a Book, What the Plus! Google+ for the Rest of Us, and Enchantment: The Art of Changing Hearts, Minds, and Actions. Kawasaki has a BA from Stanford University and an MBA from UCLA as well as an honorary doctorate from Babson College.

http://www.guykawasaki.com/enchantment/pictures/

If you're interested in having me speak at an event, please contact Keynote Speakers at info@keynotespeakers.com or call 650-325-8711.

Description

I share enchanting stuff. All the time. In large quantities.

The topics that I focus on are self-publishing, marketing, enchantment, social media, entrepreneurship, innovation, venture capital, science, and photography. I publish approximately five-ten posts per day.

Sign up here to receive my HASO email list: http://bit.ly/1e0n2Kq...
See More

6. Tell Your Story

In addition to an avatar, platforms permit a second, larger photo, called a "cover" (Facebook, Google+, and LinkedIn) or a "header" (Twitter). Its purpose is to tell a story and communicate information about what's important to you.

This is where you can show a photo of your family, dog, car, product, or passion.

Platforms change the optimal dimensions of avatars and cover/header photos all the time, so we monitor what the platforms do and regularly update in a blog post called "Quick Tips for Great Social Media Graphics." Refer back to it whenever you want to know what's optimal.

The cover is also a place where you can blow your social-media credibility by not changing the default design that platforms provide. If you don't add a custom photo, you are screaming that you are clueless about social media. (There's an entire chapter about cluelessness coming up.)

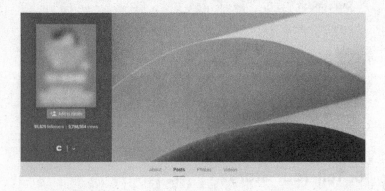

You can have more fun and display more creativity with your cover photo than with your avatar. You can also change it more often. With my cover photo, I'm trying to tell a story that I am significant enough to make speeches.

7. Get a Vanity URL

You can get a vanity URL for your Google+, Facebook, or LinkedIn account. That means people will see this kind of link:

https://plus.google.com/+GuyKawasaki/posts

If you don't get a vanity URL, people will see this kind of link, which is much harder to remember:

https://plus.google.com/+112374836634096795698/posts

Here are the instructions for Google+, Facebook, and LinkedIn. Like domain names, it's too late to get many vanity URLs, but almost anything is better than twenty-one random numbers. Also, coming up with a vanity URL is a good test of your cleverness, so an inability or unwillingness to do so impugns your intellectual prowess.

8. Finish the Job

People will make a snap decision based on your avatar, tagline, and cover/header photo and will subsequently follow, learn more about, or ignore you. If they decide to follow or learn more, they will read the rest of your profile. That is why you need to complete your profile. Google+, for example, enables you to provide introductory text, contact information, and links.

9. Go Pro

Everyone and everything on Facebook has an "account." Each account has a personal "Timeline," and it can also manage "Pages." Your personal Timeline can have up to five thousand "friends" and unlimited "followers" who can see your public posts. Pages can have unlimited "likes," and they support more types of ads. You can read about the differences between Timelines and Pages here.

Google+ has similar conventions. "Profiles" are for individuals, and "pages" are for commercial entities, celebrities, and artists. You can read about the differences between these "identities" here.

If you're going to use social media for business, you have

Story

Tagline
I empower people.

Introduction
Chief evangelist of Canva, an online graphic design tool. Formerly, advisor to the CEO of Motorola and chief evangelist of Apple. I have written twelve books including *APE: Author, Publisher, Entrepreneur--How to Publish a Book*, *What the Plus! Google+ for the Rest of Us*, and *Enchantment: The Art of Changing Hearts, Minds, and Actions*. I have a BA from Stanford University and an MBA from UCLA as well as an honorary doctorate from Babson College.

I publish approximately five-ten posts per day. I focus on are design, marketing, enchantment, social media, entrepreneurship, innovation, venture capital, science, and photography.

Contact Information

Contact info

Email	guykawasaki@gmail.com ✅
Address	Silicon Valley, California

Links

Google+ URL
google.com/+GuyKawasaki

Website
Canva.com

YouTube
▶️ Guy Kawasaki

Links

🔲 APE: Author, Publisher, Entrepreneur

🅰️ Holy Kaw!

🐦 GuyKawasaki

📘 Facebook

in LinkedIn

📷 Instagram

📌 Pinterest

no choice but to use a Page/page on both platforms—for example, Facebook's terms of service warn that using a personal Timeline for business (as opposed to a Page) can result in the closure of your account.

Fortunately, Facebook enables you to <u>convert a personal Timeline to a Page</u>. You can also <u>convert a Page back to a personal Timeline</u> should you change your mind. Google+ enables you to create a new page from an account, but not to convert a profile to a page without an act of God.

Generally speaking, you should go pro with a page if you're using social media for business, because of added capabilities such as multiple administrators and extensive analytics. For Google+ in particular, sharing posts with external services such as Buffer, Sprout Social, and Hootsuite is much, much, much better with a page.

10. Go Anonymous

When you're happy with your profile, our final recommendation is that you view it in an "incognito window." This is a browser window that hides your identity. Viewing your profile this way means that you will see it the way other people do.

To get an incognito window in Chrome, launch <u>"New Incognito Window"</u> from the File menu. There's a way to do this in every browser. Search Google for "anonymous" plus your browser name to find out how.

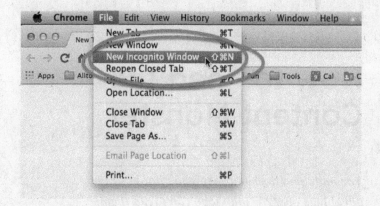

2

How to Feed the Content Monster

The man who does not read good books has no advantage over the man who can't read them.

MARK TWAIN

The biggest daily challenge of social media is finding enough content to share. We call this "feeding the Content Monster." There are two ways to do this: content creation and content curation.

Content creation involves writing long posts, taking pictures, or making videos. Our experience is that it's difficult to create more than two pieces of content per week on a sustained basis, and two pieces are not enough for social media. Helping you master content creation is outside the scope of this book.

Content curation involves finding other people's good stuff, summarizing it, and sharing it. Curation is a win-win-win: you need content to share; blogs and websites need more traffic; and people need filters to reduce the flow of information. Helping you feed—indeed satiate—the Content Monster is the purpose of this chapter.

11. Make a Plan

I'm not a believer in planning if you define *planning* as spending six months cogitating on or hiring an agency to map out and achieve strategic goals. However, most people need a tactical, logical, and cogent plan to support what they want to accomplish with social media. The gist of planning for social media and all content marketing is simple:

1. Figure out how to make money.
2. Figure out what kind of people you need to attract to make money.
3. Figure out what those people want to read (which is probably different from what you want them to read).

12. Use an Editorial Calendar

I'm not a believer in calendaring because I subscribe to the "spray and pray" theory of social media (that is, throw out a lot of stuff and hope something works). I only need to know when Peg needs content—as Jack Bauer only needs to know when he has to get the bad guys in twenty-four hours.

Peg, on the other hand, is a planner to the point of being obsessive-compulsive. She uses an editorial calendar to help manage blog posts and their accompanying social-media promotion. She also uses it to manage Google+, Facebook, and LinkedIn posts. According to Peg, several tools can help you manage an editorial calendar.

- **Excel.** You can use this old standby product to store draft posts according to the date of publication.

- **Google Docs.** The strength of <u>Google Docs</u> for social-media calendaring is that you can collaborate with team members in real time, and everyone can access the calendar from many devices. This eliminates the need for back-and-forth e-mailing and also reduces the likelihood of changes getting lost.

- **HubSpot editorial calendar.** This is an Excel template that was designed for a team to calendar social-media activities. The <u>HubSpot editorial calendar</u> can act as a guide to brainstorm ideas for your blog, monitor the content, and track the progress of your writers. You can add keywords, themes, and calls to action for each post. You cannot, however, share from the HubSpot editorial calendar because it's an Excel template.

- **Buffer, Sprout Social, and Hootsuite.** All three of these services provide calendaring functionality that's oriented toward sharing posts. Buffer is a scheduling-only platform, so you can't monitor your posts for activity. Sprout Social and Hootsuite allow you to schedule and monitor your social media, as well as to comment and respond. (Disclosure: I advise Buffer.)

- **Stresslimit.** This WordPress plug-in enables you to plan your blog content and review what's scheduled for the future.

13. Pass the Reshare Test

It's nice when people "like" and "+1" your posts. It's swell when people comment. These actions are akin to tipping a waiter or waitress.

However, resharing your posts is the ultimate compliment, because it means that people are risking their reputations on what you've written. This is akin to recommending that your friends eat at a restaurant as opposed to simply leaving a tip. Resharing is caring!

You read it here first. The key test for the art and science of social media is this:

Will people reshare my post?

Every time you share something, it should pass this test. Resharing, not imitation, is the sincerest form of flattery on social media.

14. Reshare Your Pals' Posts

Theoretically, you follow people because of the quality of what they share. Therefore, it makes sense to watch what they share, cherry-pick the best stuff, and share it too. If you don't reshare much of their stuff, it means you're following the wrong people.

15. Piggyback on Curation and Aggregation Services

Many services provide good content using techniques that range from manual curation to black magic. These are our favorite sources.

Alltop

Alltop is an aggregation of topics ranging from A (adoption) to Z (zoology). Alltop researchers select RSS feeds from thousands of websites and blogs and organize them into more than a thousand topics. For example, there's food, photography, Macintosh, travel, and adoption.

You can personalize Alltop by creating a customized collection of RSS feeds. Here is <u>my personalized Alltop collection of sites</u>. I use it almost every day to find content. You're welcome to use it too. (Disclosure: I am one of the cofounders of Alltop.)

The Big Picture *and* In Focus

These sites represent Alan Taylor's vision of how to create photo essays about current events. He started with *The Big Picture* as an online feature for the *Boston Globe* and then moved to *In Focus* at the *Atlantic*. The content of both sites is always top-notch.

Buffer

Buffer enables you to schedule posts to Google+, LinkedIn, Facebook, and Twitter. It also suggests stories to share.

Feedly

Feedly is an RSS-feed aggregator that collects information from blogs and websites and presents it in a magazine format. Flipboard is a similar product.

Futurity

The basis for many stories in mainstream news is press releases from universities. Futurity enables you to scoop the press, because it publishes research findings from a consortium of universities. An easy way to access Futurity is to use Futurity.alltop.

Google Scholar

I got this tip from <u>Belle Beth Cooper</u>, a talented social-media blogger. She searches for topics using <u>Google Scholar</u>, a subset of the Google search engine, to find serious academic treatment of topics. For example, here are the search results for "<u>persuasion</u>."

Holy Kaw

<u>Holy Kaw</u> is part of the Alltop website. Several very good curators look for human-interest stories that make people say "Holy cow!" (Holycow.com was taken, but since *Kawasaki* is pronounced "*cow*-asaki," I thought "Holy Kaw" would work.) You can find something worth sharing every day on Holy Kaw.

Klout

<u>Klout</u> measures the strength of people's reputations based on their social-media power. In 2014, it repositioned itself to help people "create and share great content." It does this by suggesting stories that people can share.

LinkedIn Influencers and Pulse

The <u>LinkedIn Influencer</u> program comprises several hundred leaders who share high-quality long-form posts. This program is closed to new applicants, but it's worth following participants for their content.

LinkedIn Pulse provides curated business content. There's also a LinkedIn Pulse app <u>for iOS</u> and <u>Android</u>. You can follow specific channels on LinkedIn, LinkedIn Influencers, and other websites.

NPR

<u>National Public Radio (NPR)</u> delivers great content every day—remarkably so. My favorite shows are *Tech Nation*, *Fresh Air*, and *Wait Wait . . . Don't Tell Me!* You can always find something on NPR that's worth sharing, unless you believe that climate change is a myth, women shouldn't have equal rights, and everyone needs an automatic weapon. <u>NPR .alltop</u> is a handy way to access NPR.

Reddit

<u>Reddit</u> bills itself as "the front page of the Internet." People vote for stories, and the site displays the most popular ones on its home page. There are also "subreddits" for specific topics, such as gaming, news, and movies, so that you can find popular stories in narrower subjects. The content skews toward a male, tech-oriented audience.

SmartBrief

SmartBrief curates high-quality content for trade associa-
tions, and since there is a trade association for almost every
industry, it covers many topics. It's easy to tap into Smart-
Brief's content because it publishes summaries of its cura-

tion. For example, to find stories about social media, use the <u>social-media SmartBrief page</u>.

StumbleUpon

StumbleUpon is a community of people who "stumble upon" and rate the quality of websites. This action enters the pages into the StumbleUpon system for the rest of the community to access. StumbleUpon <u>categorizes websites,</u> so members can select from topics such as gadgets, design, and sports.

TED

TED produces some of the most intellectually stimulating videos in the world. Its eighteen-minute limit forces speakers to get to the point. The expansion of TED to local and regional conferences has made this source even richer. You can subscribe to the <u>TED YouTube</u> and <u>TEDx YouTube</u> channels to receive notifications of new videos and stay ahead of most people.

16. Share What's Already Popular

This may feel like cheating, but it helps feed the Content Monster. There are many ways to discover what's already popular and to share these stories. For example, something that's trending on StumbleUpon might not have hit Google+ yet.

Don't worry about sharing something that "everyone" has already seen, because there are billions of people and millions of stories. Reliance on this technique can dull your personal voice and perspective, however, so don't allow it to dominate your curation.

Here are five sources that work for us.

Most-Popular.alltop

Most-Popular.alltop aggregates the most popular and most e-mailed stories from sources such as the *New York Times*, the BBC, CBS, NPR, and the *Los Angeles Times*. I created this Alltop topic because I found myself tapping the wisdom of the crowd and sharing the most popular and most e-mailed stories that people selected.

What's Hot on Google

"What's hot" tracks the most popular posts on Google+. The good news/bad news is that this feed appears to be customized for individuals. Thus you might want to read the stories in What's hot, but not necessarily want to share them.

Also, while we're on Google, there's Google Trends, which displays what types of information people are searching for around the world. You can specify the country and create personalized subscriptions for topics of interest.

Trending Topics on Facebook

The right side of your News Feed in Facebook contains an area called "Trending." This is also a useful source for stories to share.

Popular Pins on Pinterest

You can spot current trends and hot stories by looking at the <u>popular pins on Pinterest</u>. The content here tends toward fashion and food. This is Peg's go-to site for her personal accounts.

Pinterest's "guided search" provides interesting content by progressively refining your search. For example, I did a search for "hockey," then added "wedding" and "cakes," and ended up with these results. Try the same search in Google, and you'll see that the results are not as interesting.

Evergreen Topics

There are some topics that are almost always popular. I don't mean "funny cats" and "cute puppies," but ones that are a skosh more substantive and cerebral. Here's a list of a few of them:

- Coffee
- George Takei
- LEGO
- NASA (h/t Wayne Brett)
- *Star Trek* (h/t Danielle M. Villegas)
- *Star Wars* (h/t Mike Allton)

You shouldn't make these types of posts the core of your curation, but adding something fun a few times a week will make your account more interesting to follow.

(Note: We use "h/t" (hat tip) throughout the book to

give credit to our sources. Sometimes Peg uses "tiara tip" as a variation in her posts.)

17. Use Lists, Circles, Communities, and Groups

People and organizations that share a common interest comprise "lists" (Twitter and Facebook), "circles" (Google+), "communities" (Google+), and "groups" (Facebook and LinkedIn). These groupings are a powerful way to tap into good content.

Twitter Lists

A Twitter list is a grouping of Twitter accounts, usually by shared interest or expertise. Here is a list of the <u>top 100 users discussing social media</u> and a list that Peg compiled of <u>social-media tweets</u>. To find more topics, search <u>for Twitter lists</u>. You can also <u>create your own</u>.

There are public and private Twitter lists. Use a public list if you want to find interesting users for a topic such as blogging, tech news, or entrepreneurship. Use a private list (accessible only to the creator) to track, for example, what competitors are doing and what people are saying about them.

Facebook Lists

You can build lists of Facebook people and organizations who share your interests and also follow other people's lists. You don't have to "like" a Page or follow a person to put the Page or person on one of your lists. To find lists to use, go to your "Interests" Page and click on "Add interests" at the top of the Page. Learn more about <u>Facebook lists here</u>.

Google+ Circles

In Google+ people create "circles" as a way to organize their contacts. Here is a <u>circle of photographers</u> curated by <u>Thomas Hawk</u>, a very popular photographer on Google+. You can search for Google+ circles in <u>this Google doc</u> and then use them to find people to add to your circles. Here's how to <u>create circles</u>.

Google+ Communities

People interact on a peer-to-peer basis in Google+ communities. There are public and private (controlled-admittance) communities. For example, this is a <u>mobile-device community</u> that I started when I was advising Motorola, and this is a <u>street photographers community</u>. You can <u>search for communities</u>, and you can also <u>set up a community</u>.

Facebook and LinkedIn Groups

There are two kinds of groups: public and private. Anyone can join a public group and view the content. A private group is by invitation only, and only members can see the content.

LinkedIn groups are for networking and connecting with professionals in the same industry, and Facebook groups run the gamut of personal topics, such as high school reunion groups, colleges hosting incoming groups of freshmen, and fan groups to discuss common interests. Here's a <u>directory of LinkedIn groups</u>.

Google+ Search

You would expect that a social-media platform from Google would have powerful search capabilities, and you'd be right. Google+ allows you to search by keyword and will display people, pages, and communities that match your search. In the following example, I searched on "Fujifilm X100S" and clicked on the "Communities" tab to find relevant communities.

Even if you do not use Google+, you can tap Google+ circles and communities as curation sources. I mention this because some idiot might tell you that Google+ is a "ghost town" (which it isn't) and that you shouldn't bother using it.

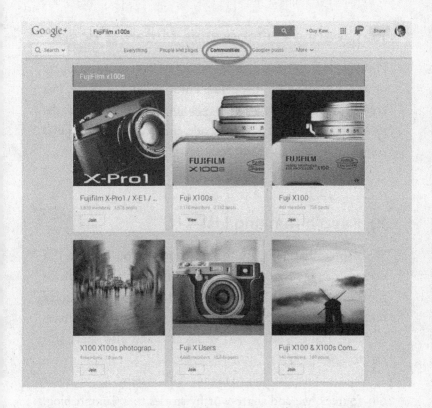

Google+ is one of the best sources of content, as well as one of the most enjoyable platforms to use, because there are fewer spammers, trolls, and idiots.

18. Create a Collaborative Pinterest Board

Pinterest boards are a rich resource for content if you create or join a board with discerning curators. For example, Peg created a board for <u>Google+ resources</u> and approved the twelve board members. As a result, this board is a continual source of high-quality information.

19. Keep a Running List

With so many new ways to find content, you may need a way to manage leads. I search for content in the middle of the night when I can't sleep, or when I'm riding a stationary bike. Later I go back to these leads and select the best ones to share. Peg can see what I've selected and also share stories for me.

Peg and I use <u>Tumblr</u> to manage this system. As we check our sources, we add share-worthy stories to a Tumblr blog. The reason we use Tumblr is that there is a Chrome extension and Android's Share menu (we both use Moto X phones and Nexus 7 tablets) makes sharing to a Tumblr blog an easy four-tap process. (I've tried to figure out how to do this with iOS but have failed.)

At one point, Peg and I decided to share our leads so that

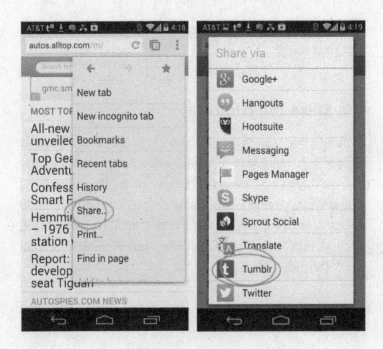

other people could benefit from our curation. We made a Tumblr blog called <u>HASO</u> (Help a Socialist Out). (Yes, we are trying to redefine the word *socialist*.) You can visit the blog or <u>subscribe to our HASO newsletter</u> if you want to see what stories we consider worth sharing.

There are other ways to keep a running list, such as a Google+ circle that has only one person (you) in it or a private Pinterest board. No matter how you do it, when you begin to actively curate stories, you may need a way to manage your leads.

20. Seize the (Holi)Day

Timing your posts to coincide with holidays and popular events is an easy way to curate great material. For example, we shared a collection of quotes called "10 Inspirational Quotes for Mother's Day," and people viewed it 165,000 times. Content geared toward major holidays and events, such as the World Cup, Earth Day, and Fashion Week, all work (h/t Julie Connor).

21. Add RSS Feeds

You can add the RSS feeds of your favorite blogs and websites to Buffer, Sprout Social, or Hootsuite to pre-populate posts. This will place every story in the feeds into a queue for sharing. With Buffer and Sprout Social, you make the final decision on a story-by-story basis. With Hootsuite, you can share every story if you use an Atom feed, or you can make a manual decision with an RSS feed.

22. Take Advantage of User-Generated Content

Share photos that others take of your products and services. This practice is good for everyone: you get social proof when someone takes note of your product or service, and the photographer receives more views and some warm and fuzzy attention that makes him or her like you even more.

Here's an extreme example: I posted the following picture of the Reset button of the Audi A3's trip odometer.

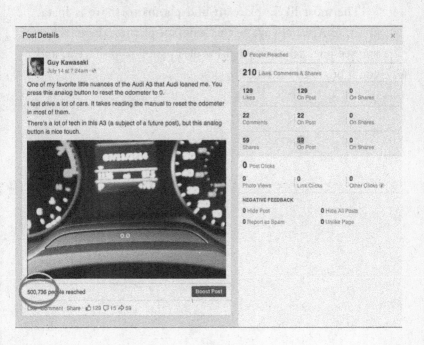

Audi USA reshared it. Then Audi dealers reshared it too. After five days, there were more than 500,000 views. Similar posts that Audi USA and Audi dealers did not reshare received only 5,000 views.

In the spirit of full disclosure, this wasn't as serendipitous as it might seem. Audi USA had sent me the A3 to review, and after I shared this picture, I sent Audi a link to it—although I'm sure Audi USA would have found it anyway. The bottom line is that both of us were happy with the results.

The most likely place to find photos to share is Instagram, so ABC (always be checking) for pictures there. When you see one, ask the owner for permission to reshare it, and you'll be off to the races.

3

How to Perfect
Your Posts

A scrupulous writer, in every sentence that he writes,
will ask himself at least four questions, thus:
1. What am I trying to say?
2. What words will express it?
3. What image or idiom will make it clearer?
4. Is this image fresh enough to have an effect?

GEORGE ORWELL, "POLITICS AND THE ENGLISH LANGUAGE"

Sharing posts gets your content creation and curation out to the world. At its foundation, social media is simple: if you share good stuff, people will reshare it, and you'll get more interaction and more followers. Everything else is optimization (or delusion).

This chapter explains what it takes to create perfect posts that will add value to the lives of your followers, build your platform, and spread your story. Peg and I advocate the most aggressive sharing practices on social media, so buckle your seat belt and put on your helmet.

23. Be Valuable

First, what exactly is "good stuff"? That's a fair and relevant question. Good stuff comes in four forms:

- **Information.** What happened? Example: Secretary of Defense Chuck Hagel says that he's open to reviewing the role of transgender people in the military.

- **Analysis.** What does it mean? Example: *Mother Jones* explains why Uruguayan soccer star Luis Suárez's biting incident during the World Cup was a big hygienic deal.

- **Assistance.** How can I do that? Example: CNET explains how texting to 911 works.

- **Entertainment.** What the hell? Example: Every year, two churches in Vrontados, Greece, stage a mock rocket war to celebrate Easter.

The goal is to emulate what I call the "NPR model." <u>NPR</u> provides great content 365 days a year. Every few months, NPR runs a pledge drive to raise money. The reason NPR can run pledge drives is that it provides such great value.

Your goal is to earn the privilege to run your own "pledge drive." A "pledge drive" in this context is a promotion for your organization, product, or service. If you are familiar with American radio or TV networks, the question is, Do you want to be NPR or <u>QVC</u>?

24. Be Interesting

Many people and most organizations narrowly define what's relevant and interesting to their followers. They mistakenly assume that their followers want to read about only a narrow band of subjects.

Should I share only stories about entrepreneurship, innovation, and technology? Should Peg share only stories about social media and blogging? Should Motorola share only stories about Motorola?

The answer in all three cases is no. To do so would be boring, and boring doesn't work on social media. You should think more broadly and take more chances. Here are some examples of how organizations can remain on-brand and at the same time be more interesting:

	DESIRED FOLLOWERS	EXAMPLES
Restaurant	Foodies	Atomic particles help solve wine fraud; the scientific way to cut a cake
Motorola	Android fans	The 100 best Android apps of 2014; six great Android tips
Airline	Travelers	The last drive-in theaters in America; mindful travel photography. Or you could make people happy even if you don't serve Japan.
Design agency	Marketers	Why it's okay to have an ad below a Web page's fold; key findings about retail-customer loyalty
Monster	Music and sports enthusiasts	"Weird Al" Yankovic's parody of Pharrell Williams's song "Happy"; fun/scary jumps

I predict that attracting more followers and catalyzing more interaction will validate this strategy. If you share this kind of interesting stuff, you'll earn the NPResque right to promote yourself to your followers, and your followers will help you get more followers.

25. Be Bold

Success favors the bold as well as the interesting on social media, so don't hesitate to express your feelings and agenda. For example, if you think there should be more women CEOs, share an article that supports your perspective. People voluntarily followed you; they can voluntarily unfollow you if they don't like what you share.

My theory is that if you're not pissing people off on social media, you're not using it right. Some people will complain that you share too much or share posts that are not perfect for them. This is what I refer to as "Internet Entitlement syndrome." Sufferers believe that everything should be free and perfectly tailored to them, because they are the center of the universe—Copernicus be damned.

There's much less leeway for organizations to be bold, although they can take strong stands on issues that affect them and their customers. For example, American tech firms can be bold about issues such as work visas for foreign citizens, and Planned Parenthood can be bold about pro-choice issues. But there are too many downsides, and it doesn't make sense, for example, for Apple to be bold about gun control.

26. Be Brief

Brevity beats verbosity on social media. You're competing with millions of posts every day. People make snap judgments and move right along if you don't capture their interest quickly.

Our experience is that the sweet spot for posts of *curated* content is two or three sentences on Google+ and Facebook and one hundred characters on Twitter. The sweet spot for *created* content is five hundred to a thousand words.

27. Be Thankful

Your created-content posts might not contain links, but when you're curating, by definition you're using outside sources. Every post should contain a link to your story's source. Here's what these links accomplish:

- Enable readers to learn more from the source
- Send traffic to the source as an act of gratitude
- Increase your visibility and popularity with bloggers and websites

When you find content because of someone else's post, use this protocol: compose and share a post with a link to the source and then add a "hat tip" to the person who brought it to your attention.

28. Be Visual

Every post—literally every single post—should contain "eye candy" in the form of a picture, graphic, or video. According to a study by Skyword, "On average, total views [of its clients' content] increased by 94% if a published article contained a relevant photograph or infographic when compared to articles without an image in the same category."

A great graphic or embedded video is as important for the success of a post as the text. Here are several ways to be visual:

- **Include a link to the story.** On Google+ and Facebook, including a link automatically brings in a photo from the story. Beware that these pictures are smaller than the maximum allowable size and are postage-stamp size on Google+.

- **Take a screenshot or "Save As" a picture from the source and manually add it to the post.** Try to get a picture that is at least 500 pixels wide. Beware that you'll be treading on tricky fair use and copyright territory when you do this. The University of Minnesota

<u>provides a checklist</u> to help determine whether you're in the clear; you're probably not, because your use is commercial (not transformative), substantial, and likely to reduce the salability of the photo. Also Facebook prefers that you use the link method rather than a manual upload.

- **Create your own graphics using <u>Canva</u>, the company that I work for.** Canva provides templates, vector graphics, fonts, and $1-per-use stock photos to make your life easier.

No matter how you get your photos and graphics, you should always try to use the optimal size for each platform. We constantly monitor the platforms and update <u>this blog post</u> for you.

29. Be Organized

If your post on Google+, Facebook, or LinkedIn is longer than four paragraphs, try to use a bulleted or numbered list. This makes it easier to read, because the information is organized into smaller chunks, and it reduces the tl;dr (too long; didn't read) effect.

Maybe I'm the only person in the world who does this, but I tune out when there's paragraph after paragraph of text. If I want to read a novel, I'll buy an e-book. I am much more likely to read a post that has a bulleted or numbered list.

30. Be Sly

I find posts that are titled "How to . . . ," "Top Ten . . . ,"
or "The Ultimate . . ." irresistible. These words say to me,
This is going to be practical and useful. The folks at <u>Twelve-
skip</u> compiled the following infographic of seventy-four
great titles, so be sly and use it.

Here's my top 10 from the infographic on the next page:

1. How to Rock ___
2. Quick Guide___
3. A Complete Guide to___
4. Questions You Should Ask Before___
5. Rules for___
6. Essential Steps to___
7. Most Popular Ways to___
8. Tips for Busy___
9. Tactics to___
10. What No One Tells You About___

31. Be Found

Hashtags are a beautiful thing. They connect posts from
people all over the world and add structure to an otherwise

74 CLEVER BLOG POST TITLE TEMPLATES THAT WORK

1. How To _____ That Drives _____
2. How To _____ in [#] easy steps
3. How To _____ In _____
4. How I Made _____ In _____
5. How To Find _____
6. How To Rock _____
7. How To Make A Strong _____
8. How To Completely Change _____
9. How To Create _____ That Gets _____
10. How To Use _____ To Stand Out
11. How To Tell If _____
12. How To _____ The Right Way
13. How _____ Can Inspire Your _____
14. How To Get Rid Of _____
15. What To Do With _____
16. Where To Find _____
17. Quick Guide: _____
18. A Complete Guide To _____
19. Ultimate Guide: _____
20. Beginners Guide: _____
21. Hack: _____
22. DIY: _____
23. The Anatomy Of _____ That Gets _____
24. [#] Things your _____ Doesn't Tell You
25. [#] _____ Trends For [YEAR]
26. [#] _____ Every _____ Should Own
27. [#] _____ To Consider For _____
28. [#] Amazing _____ To Try Right Now
29. [#] Insane _____ That Will Give You _____
30. [#] Types Of _____
31. [#] Questions You Should Ask Before _____
32. [#] Worth-It _____ For _____
33. [#] Secrets To _____
34. [#] Resources to Help You Become _____
35. [#] Signs You Might _____
36. [#]-Point Checklist: _____

37. [#] Rules For _____
38. [#] Habits Of _____
39. [#] Ideas To _____
40. [#] Trends You Need To Know _____
41. [#] Best _____ To _____
42. [#] _____ We Love
43. [#] Facts About _____
44. [#] Essential Things For _____
45. [#] Key Benefits Of _____
46. [#] Examples Of _____ To Inspire You
47. [#] _____ That Will Motivate You
48. [#] _____ Ideas
49. [#] Reasons You Didn't Get _____
50. Getting Smart With: _____
51. [#] Smart Strategies To _____
52. [#] Most Effective Tactics To _____
53. [#] Most Popular Ways To _____
54. [#] Essential Steps To _____
55. [#] Wrong Ways To _____
56. [#] Creative Ways _____
57. [#] Tips For Busy _____
58. [#] No-Nonsense _____
59. [#] Surprising _____
60. [#] Foolproof _____ Tips For _____
61. [#] Epic Formula To _____
62. [#] Handy Tips From _____ For _____
63. [#] Superb Ways To _____ Without _____
64. [#] Tricks _____
65. [#] Ways To Make Sure Your _____ Is Not _____
66. [#] Mistakes You'll Never Make Again
67. [#] Weird But Effective _____ For _____
68. [#] Tactics To _____
69. [#] Super Tips _____
70. [#] That Will Make You _____
71. [#] Supercharge Your _____
72. [#] Pleasant Ways To _____
73. [#] Wittiest _____ To _____
74. What No One Tells You About _____

MORE AT TWELVESKIP.COM // BY PAULINE CARRERA

#socialmediatips

#SocialMedia	#DigitalMarketing
#SocialMediaMarketing	#SMM
#SMDay	#SmallBusiness
#Marketing	#SocialMediaManagement
#Facebook	#LinkedIn
#Twitter	#Branding
#SocialMediaStrategy	#SocialNetworking
#Business	#MarketingTips
#Media	#Strategy
#ContentMarketing	#Content

#Explore a hashtag

Anna Godfrey
Shared publicly · 1:19 PM   #SocialMediaMarketing

Summer Special on My Basic Social Media Guide!

Social Media has taken business and network marketing to the next level! If you are new to social media for business...then this is going to help you out a lot! Lots of info found in one book!

It's amazing how the internet has made the world smaller and business opportunity bigger. To avoid the risk of becoming irrelevant in business you must become social. Social media is a way to help drive traffic to your websites, attend to customer service more personally and effectively, and keep you ahead of the marketing trends.

A good business person stays ahead of trends and are always seeking the next big thing. Some social medias come like a hurricane and you must hop on and ride through the social media influence storm. We must not count any social media out. Each platform adds something different and will have different types of users, thus expanding your reach.

Nerd Girl SEO's Guide to Basic Social Media:
http://annagodfrey.com/read-my-book/

unstructured ecosystem. When you add a hashtag to a post, you are telling people the post is relevant to a shared topic. For example, #socialmediatips on Google+ connects posts that are about social media.

Twitter, Instagram, Facebook, Tumblr, and Google+ all support hashtags, so this is a common and well-accepted practice.

We recommend adding two or three hashtags to your posts. If you use more, you look like an #idiot who's trying to #gamethesystem. Also, don't use hashtags on Pinterest, because people hate them there—perhaps because they interfere with the minimal-text sensibilities of Pinterest posts.

32. Be Active

By "active" we mean three to twenty different (that is, not repeated) posts per day. That's a guideline. As long as your posts are good, you can share more than that. But if you share one or two *crappy* posts per day, that's too much.

Admittedly, you're reading a book coauthored by someone who repeats many tweets four times. However, trust me on this one, and try sharing at the level in the "Hard-Core" column in the following chart. (The numbers include both created and curated posts.)

PLATFORM	CASUAL	HARD-CORE
Facebook	1-2	3-4
Google+	3-4	8-10
LinkedIn (short-form)	1	4
Pinterest	6	10-12
Twitter	8-12	25

The day before this book went to our copy editor, I had the brilliant idea that maybe we should check this assertion. Peg was in Australia; instead of repeating our tweets eight hours apart, we shared four identical posts with four different links to track clicks. Here are the results.

DATE AND TIME	CLICKS	RESPONSES	RETWEETS	FAVORITES
7/6, 4:41 p.m.	1,300	22	18	41
7/7, 11:28 p.m.	1,300	20	17	43
7/8, 9:50 p.m.	2,300	24	23	26
7/8, 5:00 a.m.	2,700	16	10	15
Total	7,600	82	68	125

Would you rather have 1,300 clicks or 7,600? Would you be willing to risk complaints about repeated tweets and the possibility that people might unfollow your account to achieve 5.8 times more clicks? I would—and do—every day of the year.

Some people will complain about the higher volume, but don't sweat it. They will either get used to the increase or unfollow you. What matters is the net effect: are you adding followers and gaining reshares? As I mentioned before, if you're not pissing someone off on social media, you're not using it aggressively enough.

33. Be Distributed

Using tools to schedule and distribute posts isn't cheating. It's what smart people do to optimize their sharing. Anyone who insists that you must manually share your posts is silly. Most followers can't tell how a post was shared, and if you have a life outside social media, you probably can't manually share posts throughout the day.

Here's a list of services you can use to distribute your posts. In thirty minutes, you could plan a day's worth of posts by using any of them.

- **Buffer.** This is the service that I use. It schedules posts for Google+ pages, Facebook Pages and profiles, LinkedIn, and Twitter. We like the ability to add posts at a specific time or to put them in a queue. Team management and analytics are available in the Buffer for Business plan. Buffer suggests stories to share, and it's the prettiest of the services. We like pretty.

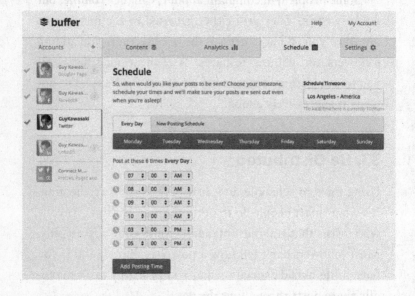

- **Do Share**. This is the only product that enables you to schedule Google+ posts if you have a personal page. It is a Chrome extension and requires that Chrome be running in order to work. Do Share is great but limited by that requirement. For example, if you're traveling and your computer isn't running, Do Share won't share your posts.

- **Friends+Me**. This service enables you to share your Google+ posts to other platforms. It currently supports Facebook (groups, profiles, and Pages), Twitter, LinkedIn (profiles, groups, and company pages), and Tumblr. We like that the image from your Google+ post appears in your tweets. Using hashtags, you can control how and where each post is shared or if you want it to post only to Google+.

- **Hootsuite**. From our friends in Canada, Hootsuite allows you to schedule content and to monitor and respond to comments. You can share to Facebook profiles and Pages, Google+ pages, LinkedIn profiles, and Twitter. Using the <u>Viraltag app</u>, you can schedule pins on Pinterest. We like the ability to bulk-schedule tweets and posts from a spreadsheet, drag and drop from the calendar for scheduling, and collaborate with teams for tweeting.

- **Post Planner**. This product works only with Facebook. It provides stories to share and also suggests when to share. With easy access from an app inside Facebook, you can find viral photos and trending content for story ideas. You can also add feeds for blogs that you like and share from Post Planner. It's a great service for managers of Facebook Pages.

- **Sprout Social.** This is Peg's favorite. It provides the ability to publish on, engage with, and monitor Facebook Pages and profiles; Twitter; Google+ pages; and LinkedIn profiles. There is team-management functionality and integration with Zendesk. We like the ability to repeat the same tweet with an image and create a team calendar. It costs a minimum of $59 per month.

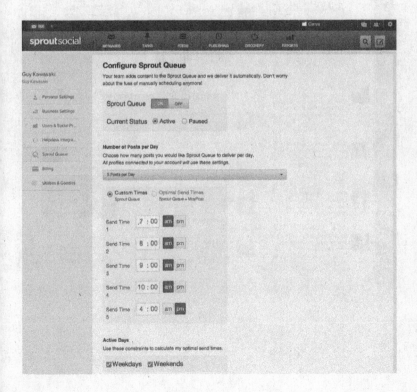

- **Tailwind.** This service provides scheduling and monitoring for Pinterest. The display of popular pins, trending boards, and other people's popular content is a powerful feature. Tailwind has access to Pinterest's application programming interface (API), so we're expecting even more features in the near future.

- **TweetDeck.** This is a stand-alone application to monitor activity and schedule tweets. It displays search results in separate columns. For example, you can create one column for personal @mentions (an @mention is when people tweet the @ symbol and your name) and another column for @mentions of your competition. The next time you go to a tech conference, look at how people are monitoring Twitter, and you'll see that most are using TweetDeck.

There are other products that provide similar functionality, including Everypost, Sendible, and SocialOomph, but we have not used any of them.

34. Be on Top

On top of the hour, that is. Jay Baer, author of *Youtility*, shares posts a few minutes before or after the top of the hour. His reasoning is that this is when people tend to check their social-media accounts because they are between meetings. (Or they are running late, so it's the least likely time for them check.) Like most social-media advice, it's hard to test scientifically, but it's worth trying.

35. Be a Mensch

"Give to others without having an agenda," says <u>Mari Smith</u>, the queen of Facebook. If you share purely for the joy of helping others, the amount of goodness and reciprocity you'll receive will surprise you.

My theory is that for every one person who suffers from Internet Entitlement syndrome, there are one hundred who believe in reciprocity and acting like a mensch. A "mensch," in case you haven't heard the term before, is a kind and honorable person who does the right thing the right way.

So share other people's posts, make positive and intelligent comments, suggest resources and solutions, and rack up points on the karmic scoreboard in the clouds. Goodness will eventually flow to your posts, I promise.

36. Be Promotional

We hardly ever do this, as a matter of pride and principle, but paying to promote posts on Pinterest, Facebook, and Twitter can work. This ensures that more people will see your posts. Facebook, in particular, is becoming a "pay to play" platform.

The decision of whether to use this tactic comes down to the math: does the revenue justify the expense of paying for the views? For example, you could "pay to promote" a post with a call to action to buy your book. The additional sales (and perhaps brand awareness) may or may not be worth the cost.

Here's a post that Canva paid to promote to advertise a job opening. We geo-targeted this promoted post only to people in Australia, and you can see that $60 brought approximately 14,000 views.

If you refuse to pay to promote your posts (we'd respect you if this were your decision), you can "pin" your posts to the top of your page on Facebook and Twitter. This means that the post remains as the first visible story at the top of your Timeline. This isn't as effective as paying for promotion, but it's free.

Canva
Posted by Zach Kitschke [?] · May 15 · Edited ·

Are you an amazing designer ready to rock the world of design? We're looking for an incredible intern to join our team in Sydney, Australia.

You'll be working alongside our team of talented designers, engineers and marketers to help shape the future of design.

Know someone who'd be perfect? Tag them in this post.

Here are the details on how to apply: http://www.pedestrian.tv/jobs/design-photography/amazing-graphic-design-intern-needed-to-help-shape/087a72f5-a2f6-44b8-bce6-2d1ce22ba5ef.htm

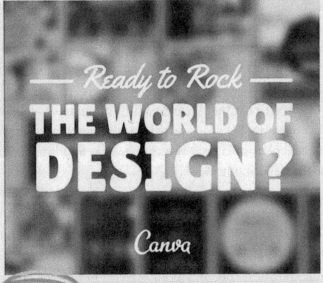

13,992 people reached   See Results ▼

Like · Comment · Share

👍 32 people like this.   Top Comments ▼

37. Be Multilingual

Héctor García translates Japanese news into Spanish, and because he's often the first person to share the news, his posts become the de facto source. This is a clever idea. If you are bilingual (or multilingual), try translating breaking news into another language and see what happens.

38. Be Analytical

You can improve the relevance of your content (while keeping in mind my exhortations to share things that are interesting and bold) by analyzing the characteristics of the people who follow you. For example, Facebook's analytics are a rich resource for finding out who your fans are, and this is a great place to start when planning future content for Facebook.

We also use LikeAlyzer to check our Facebook Pages and tweak the content, the types of posts, and when we're sharing.

Twitter provides extensive analytics for verified accounts, including the number of impressions per tweet and how many people engaged with each tweet (defined as clicking anywhere on the tweet plus retweets, replies, follows, and favorites). You can use a service such as SocialBro, which

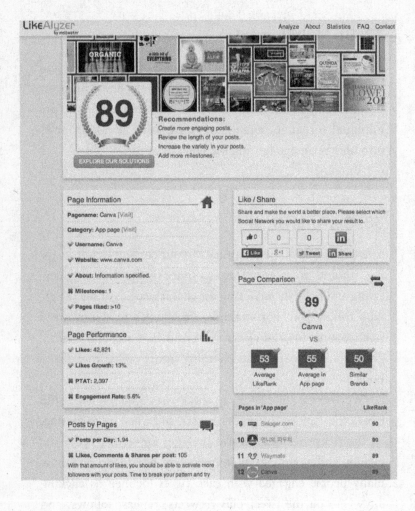

LikeAlyzer
by meltwater

Analyze About Statistics FAQ Contact

89

Recommendations:
Create more engaging posts.
Review the length of your posts.
Increase the variety in your posts.
Add more milestones.

EXPLORE OUR SOLUTIONS

Page Information 🏠

Pagename: Canva [Visit]

Category: App page [Visit]

Ⅴ **Username:** Canva

Ⅴ **Website:** www.canva.com

Ⅴ **About:** Information specified.

❇ **Milestones:** 1

Ⅴ **Pages liked:** >10

Page Performance 📊

Ⅴ **Likes:** 42,821

Ⅴ **Likes Growth:** 13%

❇ **PTAT:** 2,397

❇ **Engagement Rate:** 5.6%

Posts by Pages 💬

Ⅴ **Posts per Day:** 1.94

❇ **Likes, Comments & Shares per post:** 105
With that amount of likes, you should be able to activate more
followers with your posts. Time to break your pattern and try

Like / Share

Share and make the world a better place. Please select which
Social Network you would like to share your result to.

👍 0   0   0   in

Like   g+1   Tweet   Share

Page Comparison

89

Canva

VS

53 | 55 | 50

Average | Average in | Similar
LikeRank | App page | Brands

Pages in 'App page'		LikeRank
9	Seloger.com	90
10	언니의 파우치	90
11	Waymate	89
12	Canva	89

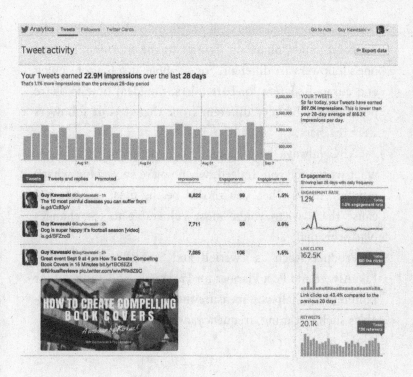

reveals who follows you, helps you find new people to follow, and illustrates how your content is doing. You can also get similar reports in Sprout Social and Hootsuite.

39. Be Curious

If you asked five social-media "experts" a question, you'd get seven different answers. Our advice is to field-test common generalizations such as "Share on Facebook on the weekend" and "Share on Twitter in the morning." Everyone's followers are different. For example, if you wrote a blog and curated content for bartenders, the ideal time to share posts would be very different from that if your followers were teachers.

ABC (always be curious) and experiment to find out what works for you. Indeed, when you're sure about what's optimal, that's when you should be the most curious, because that's when you're most vulnerable to the changes platforms make.

Products such as Tweriod and SocialBro for Twitter, LikeAlyzer and Post Planner for Facebook, and Tailwind for Pinterest can help you measure the effects of changing variables such as timing, frequency, and graphics use.

40. Be Defiant

In our opinion, most search engine optimization (SEO) is bullshit. It involves trying to read Google's mind and then gaming the system to make Google find crap. There are three thousand computer science PhDs at Google trying to make each search relevant, and then there's you trying to fool them. Who's going to win?

Tricking Google is futile. Instead, you should let Google do what it does best: find great content. So defy all the SEO witchcraft out there and focus on creating, curating, and sharing great content. This is what's called SMO: social-media optimization.

41. Be Anonymous

This is the same advice we provided earlier. You should look at your posts with an "incognito window" to double-check how other people see them.

4

How to Respond to Comments

Don't take anything personally. Nothing others do is
because of you. What others say and do is a projection
of their own reality, their own dream. When you are
immune to the opinions and actions of others,
you won't be the victim of needless suffering.

DON MIGUEL RUIZ, *THE FOUR AGREEMENTS:*
A PRACTICAL GUIDE TO PERSONAL FREEDOM

You will encounter insightful, funny, and flattering comments, and you will encounter stupid, mean, and insulting ones. The mix will be skewed toward the former if you post good stuff, but everyone gets some negative comments. If you want to use social media for business, (wo)man up and respond to comments of both kinds.

Responding to comments is hand-to-hand marketing that requires diligence and effort—there's nothing easy about it. In particular, negative comments take even more effort, patience, and understanding, and this doesn't come naturally to most people. This chapter explains how to transform responding to comments from being a pain to being a way to foster engagement, build your reputation, and even have fun.

42. Use the Right Tools

The first step is to find comments that you need to address. There are two scenarios. The first is monitoring comments in your Google+, Facebook, LinkedIn, Pinterest, and Instagram posts. Doing this is easy because these platforms organize, or "thread," the discussion, so you can share a post and go back to see if there are comments.

The second scenario is monitoring comments on Twitter. This is harder because there isn't the same level of threading. Vain as this may seem, you need to set up a search for your name—for example, @GuyKawasaki—to monitor comments about you and responses to you. You can <u>save this search</u> so that you don't need to reenter it every time.

Twitter also <u>provides advanced search capabilities</u> to make finding comments more efficient. For example, <u>here's a search</u> that finds mentions of @GuyKawasaki or @Canva, but not the retweets of our tweets. (You don't need to respond to retweets, and hopefully there will be so many that you couldn't respond to them all even if you wanted to.)

People will also make comments about you that are unrelated to your posts. You need to monitor these too. In a

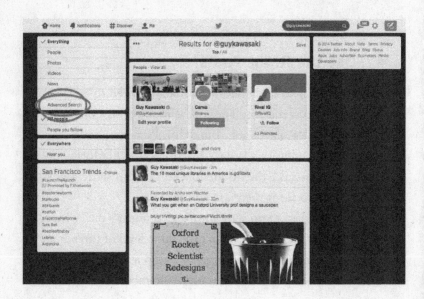

Advanced **Search**

Words

All of these words

This exact phrase

Any of these words

None of these words

These hashtags

Written in   Any Language   ⬍

People

From these accounts

To these accounts

Mentioning these accounts   @guykawasaki @canva

Places

Near this place   📍 Add location

Dates

From this date   to

Other

Select: ☐ Positive :)   ☐ Negative :(☐ Question   ☐ Include retweets

Search

perfect world, people would @mention (Twitter and Facebook) or +mention (Google+) you by typing "@" or "+" before your name. If they did, the platform would notify you via e-mail or when you were on your page. However, most people are unaware of this capability.

Many services can monitor mentions and comments, including Argyle Social, Commun.it, Google Alerts, Hootsuite, Social Mention, SocialBro, and Sprout Social. And, as mentioned before, TweetDeck is a great application for monitoring @mentions and search terms.

43. Use "Mentions," Not Hashtags

The purpose of a hashtag is to help people share a topic. This is different from a response. For example, when Audi introduces a new car and you want to discuss it with other Audi aficionados, you should use #Audi. When you make a comment about Audi or to Audi and want to ensure that Audi sees it, you should use @Audi on Facebook or Twitter and +Audi on Google+ (h/t Gary Pageau).

44. Consider the Total Audience

The audience for a response is everyone who will read it, not just the commenter. This is different from e-mail, in which the recipient and anyone he or she might forward your e-mail to are the only ones who matter.

On social media, many people might be watching and judging what you write. I would argue that the other people watching are *more* important than the original commenter. Posting on social media is analogous to a politician answering a question at a town hall meeting, and as any successful politician will tell you, everything is always on the record.

45. Assume People Are Good Until Proven Bad

As with e-mail, it's easy to misinterpret social-media comments because of their textual format. What you interpret as criticism or an attack may be innocuous or sarcastic. Or perhaps you are oversensitive.

Here's an example:

Followed by Scott McNeill and 3 others
Barry Cunningham @barrycunningham · May 13
A bigger reason than ever to converse instead of broadcast! Wonder what
@GuyKawasaki & @garyvee think about this mashable.com/2014/05/12/twi…

Mashable

Adios, Over-Tweeters: Twitter Finally Adds a Mute Button
By Mashable @mashable

View on web

Expand

Was Barry asking me this question because he thinks I
tweet too much or because he knows I dislike broadcasting?
You could interpret his tweet either way. I needed two more
tweets from him to figure out that he was simply curious
about what I thought and was not criticizing me for tweeting too much.

It's always important to look at the context in which a comment was made.

46. Stay Positive

Since others are watching, you should stay positive and pleasant no matter how banal, blasphemous, or baiting the comment. You can never go wrong by taking the high road, because winning the war for class and credibility is more important than winning the battle with one commenter. Truth be told, I sometimes forget to follow this recommendation myself, so do as I write, not as I do.

47. Agree to Disagree

If you can't stay positive (been there and done that), you can agree to disagree. There isn't always a right way, wrong way, or best way. Life is too short to be constantly fighting battles, and most battles are not worth the effort. Also, agreeing to disagree really pisses off "trolls"—online bullies who are always looking for a fight in order to compensate for inadequate organs or pathetic lives.

48. Ask the Right Question

When someone expresses a strong negative opinion, ask if he or she has firsthand experience with the issue. For example, if you shared a story about Android and an iOS fanboy attacks you, ask him if he's ever used or owned an Android phone. The odds are good that he hasn't and is only repeating what he's heard. That's the basis for how he "knows" he's right and for expressing his opinion.

On social media, the combination of certainty and ignorance is common, so get used to it! Indeed, it's often the case that the more certain a person is, the more ignorant he or she is too.

49. Go Three Rounds

The best (and worst) interactions often occur between commenters. It's enchanting to watch strangers develop relationships and take posts in deeper and serendipitous (albeit related) directions. That's the good news. The bad news is that commenters sometimes get into bitter fights and make mean-spirited comments that they would never utter in person.

My suggestion is that you embrace the rules of amateur boxing and fight for only three rounds. The opening bell is when you share a post. *Ding-ding*. Round 1: Commenter comments. Round 2: You respond. Round 3: Commenter responds to the response. End of fight.

50. Delete, Block, and Report

If all else fails, don't hesitate to ignore, delete, block, or report trolls and spammers. You don't have a moral obligation to engage with them, and there's little advantage to lowering yourself to their level. If you need help identifying someone who's a troll versus someone who's simply passionate, I've got a LinkedIn post for you.

I have a one-strike rule: I delete inappropriate comments (profanity, racism, and off-topic rabbit holes) and flag trolls and spammers on the first occurrence without hesitation. Life is too short to deal with orifices.

5

How to Integrate Social Media and Blogging

Ideas that spread, win.

SETH GODIN

A few years ago, blogging and social media were separate. Blogging was long-form, serious, and crafted. Social media was short-form, personal, and spontaneous. Some people predicted that social media would replace blogging because of declining attention spans.

I agreed with this sentiment and shifted my long-form

posts from <u>my blog</u> to Google+. Then in 2014, Peg showed me the light about the resilient value of blogging when LinkedIn created their Influencer program for long-form posts. You can see <u>my LinkedIn posts and their results here</u>.

Blogging and social media not only amicably coexist; they complement each other. The trick is to use a blog to enrich your social media with long-form posts and to use social media to promote your blog. This chapter explains how to integrate social media and blogging.

51. Curate Yourself

If someone looking for great content came across your blog, would he or she share your blog posts? We hope so. And haven't the people who've followed you expressed a desire to see your work? Logically, of all content, you should share your own blog posts. If a blog post is not worth sharing, it's not worth writing.

52. Add Drama

As I said before, every curated post should contain a picture or video, and this applies to your own posts too. Just to be clear: I'm saying that your social-media posts that link to your blog posts should have a picture. This is no time for subtlety, introversion, or modesty. If you write great stuff that informs, analyzes, assists, or entertains, you have the moral obligation to get people to notice it.

53. Add Share Buttons

Make sharing your blog posts friction-free by adding share buttons to your blog. Here's how to <u>install the Google+ button</u> and the <u>Facebook Like box</u>.

Want to Increase Blog Traffic? Some Fab Tips for Success

posted by **PEG FITZPATRICK**

Rather than adding each platform's button, you can use a product such as <u>ShareThis</u> to install multiple buttons. Also, a WordPress plug-in called <u>Flare</u> can provide a cumulative total for the number of shares across platforms. This number is a form of social proof that might encourage more people to share your posts.

54. Entice People to Follow You

Include links to your social-media accounts on your blog so that people can easily follow you. Whereas share buttons take people to specific blog posts, the links shown here take people to your social-media accounts. If your blog is interesting, people will follow you on social media, and if your social media is interesting, people will read your blog.

If you think displaying share buttons is tacky and overly promotional, look at what Tiffany & Co., the classy fine jeweler, does. If Tiffany can do it, you can too.

CUSTOMER SERVICE	LATEST FROM TIFFANY	OUR COMPANY	RELATED TIFFANY SITES
US 800 843 3269	Catalogues	Corporate Responsibility	Wedding & Gift Registry
Your Account		Investors	Business Accounts
Email Customer Service	Facebook	Tiffany Careers	Tiffany for the Press
Frequently Asked Questions	Instagram	Accessibility	Mobile Site
Shipping & Returns	Pinterest		
Product Care	Twitter		Engagement Ring Finder App for iPhone®
Privacy Policy	Tumblr		Engagement Ring Finder App for Android™
Terms Of Use	YouTube		What Makes Love True App
	Google+		The Tiffany & Co. Foundation

55. Add a ClickToTweet Link

A service called <u>ClickToTweet</u> enables you to embed a link in your blog posts and e-mails. When people click on this link, they are presented with a draft tweet. They can edit this draft or tweet it immediately.

Our experience is that many people will click on a Click-toTweet link, we think for two reasons. First, it can be an

---

clicktotweet   Tour   Downloads   Basic Link   Help   Welcome, PegFitzpatrick

Create Basic Link

You can create as many of these links as you want, but they are not tracked and stats are not recorded for them.

Message you would like tweeted

Create a quick link that you can add in a blog post with clicktotweet.

69 characters left.

Generate New Link

easy way to generate a good tweet if your content is good. Second, it's a way to thank you for your efforts.

Be sure to try this, because it's very effective.

56. Pin Every Post

Peg taught me that you should make a Pinterest post for every blog post. When people re-pin a Pinterest post, it appears in the public timeline again. Thus pins have a long shelf life, as they "reincarnate" and drive more traffic to your blog post. Nothing has the staying power of a Pinterest post.

57. Add a "Pin It for Later" Option

Many people pin articles to remind themselves to read the articles later or to collect them for future reference. You can make this easy by adding a link to your blog post with a call to action that says "Pin it for later" and that points to the article's pin.

Peg Fitzpatrick
Shared publicly · May 15, 2014   #Bullying

12 Most Sensible Ways to Deal with Online Bullies and Trolls
Tips from some some experienced online folks

Voltaire once said, "I do not agree with what you have to say, but I'll defend to the death your right to say it." from **+Dr. Julie Connor**

+Chris Brogan
"I thank them and let them be mostly. I delete their comments if they are distasteful but not if they're just negative."

+Aaron Lee
"One thing I learned is that **trolls love attention** and they would do anything to get it. I quickly learned that the best way to handle them is to either ignore them or just simply respond them with sarcasm. One of the big "no-no's" for me is don't waste your time arguing with them, because that would keep them coming back for more."

+Rebel Brown
"I bite my keyboard and then ignore them."

How do you handle trolls or online bullies?

Read it all here: http://12most.com/2012/10/09/12-ways-deal-online-bullies-trolls/

Pin it for later: http://www.pinterest.com/pin/232779874464330788/

#bullying #Trolls #ns

58. Add Your Blog to Alltop

Alltop is an RSS-feed aggregation site that helps people scan the news and find content. You can submit your blog's RSS feed to get it on an Alltop page. The process is free, so there's little downside. For example, if you want to position yourself as an expert on adoption, you should submit your blog for consideration in <u>Adoption.alltop</u>. Go <u>here to submit your blog</u> for any Alltop topic.

59. Start an E-mail List

Old-school e-mail lists remain a powerful marketing tool. If I had a choice of someone either following me on a social-media platform or subscribing to my e-mail list, I would pick the e-mail list any day. This is because I am more confident that a person will read an e-mail than see a post.

We use a product called <u>MailChimp</u> for our e-mail lists. Here are some tips for creating effective e-mails:

- **Create a custom graphic.** Pure text is boring, so add one graphic to your e-mail. More than one graphic, however, makes an e-mail look like direct-marketing spam.

- **Perfect the subject line.** The subject line of this type of e-mail is equivalent to the headline of a blog post. It must grab people. "How to . . . ," "Top Ten . . . ," and "Loved Your Book" all work on me. Refer back to the seventy-four great titles in the Twelveskip infographic in chapter 3.

- **Keep it short.** The ideal length of an e-mail is fewer than five sentences that explain who, what, why, and when—in that order. Think haiku, not *War and Peace*.

- **Provide a complete signature.** A signature is the area at the bottom of an e-mail that contains the writer's contact information. Be sure you provide your title, e-mail address, and phone number, along with icons that link to your blog and social-media accounts. Wise-Stamp is one service that creates excellent e-mail signatures.

- **Cut the quotations.** If people want inspirational quotes, they can buy those framed posters advertised in airline magazines or use Wikiquote. Be brief and stay on track with your e-mail.

- **Don't spam people.** Obey the guidelines for sending e-mail only to people who request it. MailChimp provides a good summary of antispam laws.

60. Don't Forget LinkedIn

You often don't hear LinkedIn mentioned as a social-media platform because people think of it as a site for job searches and business development. As I mentioned earlier, however, Peg showed me that LinkedIn is a powerful, pleasant, and valuable social-media platform.

Discover more

Influencers
Insights from top industry leaders

Richard Branson
Founder at Virgin Group
4,503,030 followers

Jack Welch
Executive Chairman, Jack
Welch Management Institu...
3,051,497 followers

**Deepak Chopra MD
(official)**
Founder, Chopra Foundation
3,429,890 followers

Arianna Huffington
President and Editor-in-Chief
at The Huffington Post Me...
2,805,695 followers

Bill Gates
Co-chair, Bill & Melinda
Gates Foundation
2,561,410 followers

Jeff Weiner
CEO at LinkedIn
2,080,380 followers

James Caan
Serial Entrepreneur and
Investor In People with...
1,827,241 followers

Daniel Goleman
Author of The Triple Focus: A
New Approach to Education
1,823,751 followers

David Cameron
Prime Minister of the United
Kingdom
1,389,603 followers

Gretchen Rubin
Bestselling writer about
habits and happiness...
1,265,326 followers

Guy Kawasaki
Chief Evangelist at Canva
1,203,030 followers

Barack Obama
President of the United
States of America
1,197,818 followers

T. Boone Pickens
Founder, Chairman and CEO
at BP Capital and TBP...
1,121,636 followers

Katya Andresen
CEO at Cricket Media/ePals
1,066,186 followers

Tim Brown
CEO at IDEO
975,752 followers

This is because there are hundreds of millions of people on LinkedIn who understand the usefulness of this platform for their careers. People don't make as many inappropriate posts and comments there because they are not hiding behind fictitious identities and they know that stupid moves can affect their job prospects.

You can see what "influential" people on LinkedIn are posting by <u>clicking on their pictures here</u>. The high quality of the content and the large number of followers are impressive. Also, there's a wonderful absence of people who become famous for appearing in a sex video, getting arrested for drunk driving, or committing spousal abuse.

61. Write Guest Posts

Guest posts for websites such as *HuffingtonPost*, <u>HubSpot</u>, and <u>MarketingProfs</u> can expose you to new audiences. They are a powerful option if you don't have time to maintain your own blog or you have a special event that you want to promote beyond your own subscribers and readers.

In addition to these large websites, you should contact other websites and blogs that might be interested in your guest post. You may be surprised to learn that many are desperate to get more content. I get pitched every day, so let me give you some tips on how to make an effective pitch.

- **Ensure that your post is spot-on relevant.** Many pitches leave me wondering why the writer or publicist thinks I would publish such a post.

- **Don't send a canned e-mail to multiple blogs and websites.** I can spot spraying and praying in the first line. Example: "I'm writing to suggest a fascinating business story for the Open Forum blog: 'How to Make $75 Billion This Year by Speeding Up Your Website.'"

- **Attach a draft with the pitch.** Don't make me go through a multistep dance to read your draft. I will lose interest after two e-mails.

- **Don't make me edit your writing.** I'm looking for a quick win that involves a minimum amount of work. If I have to do a lot of work, I might as well write the post myself.

- **Don't use a PR firm to make the pitch.** Do it yourself, or don't do it at all. If it's important that you place your post with me, ask me yourself. If it's not important enough for you to ask me directly, why should I share it?

62. Use SlideShare

SlideShare is the unsung hero of viral content. A popular SlideShare can attract tens of thousands of views. We recommend that you repurpose your most popular blog posts and convert them into SlideShare presentations.

For example, we conducted a wildly popular webinar for <u>Mari Smith</u> called <u>"The Perfect Post,"</u> and the <u>Slide-Share show</u> afterward was very popular as well. SlideShare presentations look fantastic when you tweet them, pin them, or share them on LinkedIn.

63. Join Blogging Networks

Blogging networks are groups of bloggers who share one another's stories. This amplifies each member's social reach. For example, <u>Triberr</u> pulls in your blog's RSS feed and shares your posts with people in your "tribe." Tribe members in turn share your posts with their social networks. Peg has 30,500 Twitter followers but can reach a total of 9 million people through the members of her tribe.

64. Embed Your Posts in Your Blog

Embedding your social-media posts in your blog is a good way to add more followers. (Here are instructions <u>from Facebook</u>, <u>Twitter</u>, <u>Google+</u>, <u>SlideShare</u>, and <u>YouTube</u>.) This

creates a richer experience within your blog and gives your readers an easy way to find you on social-media platforms.

65. Enable Social Log-in

Social log-in enables people to sign in to your website or service by using their credentials from Twitter, Facebook, Google+, and other platforms. According to Mike Stelzner of <u>Social Media Examiner</u>, this provides faster and easier registration, integration of existing avatars, display of contact information, and reduction of spam, because people are usually authenticated (h/t <u>Silvino Santos</u>).

66. Meet People in Real Life

Social media can help you start, build, and maintain relationships with people all over the world. But meeting people face-to-face can make your relationship even stronger and better. Therefore, you should attend conferences and meetups whenever you can (h/t <u>Michelle Kay</u>).

Conferences are a great place to meet many people at once, but smaller groups such as tweetups for Twitter and Hangouts in Real Life (H.I.R.L.s) for Google+ work well too. For example, Google+ members often conduct photo walks with people they meet online. This is <u>a video of a photo walk in San Francisco</u> with artist Trey Ratcliff. It provides a sense of how fun these activities are.

Photo credit: <u>Peter Adams</u>.

And this is Peg meeting her online friend <u>Jodi Okun</u> at the <u>BlogHer 2013</u> conference in one of the best photobombs ever:

67. "Peg" Your Post

From this day forth, "Peg" is a verb that means totally integrating social media and blogging. These are the ten steps Peg uses to promote a blog post:

1. Write multiple interesting and click-worthy versions of the blog title.
2. Create three images in Canva: 735 by 1102 pixels, 788 by 940 pixels, and 512 by 1024 pixels.

3. Pin the 735-by-1102-pixel image on Pinterest with two links (one in the description field and one in the source field) back to the blog post. Embed the pin in your blog post with the <u>Pinterest widget</u>.

4. Share the link to your post on LinkedIn with the 788-by-940-pixel image. Make sure the image name matches the title of your post, because LinkedIn shows the image name—for example, "image819809754.jpg" is awkward.

5. Create a longer post on Google+ with the 735-by-1102-pixel image, a link to the blog, and a link to your Pinterest post.

6. Share a short post on your Facebook profile and Page with the 788-by-940-pixel image. Add a question to start the conversation on Facebook, along with two links—one to the blog and one to the Pinterest post.

7. Tweet the blog post with the 512-by-1024-pixel image.

8. Schedule additional tweets with quotes from the post using the different titles.

9. Share your article in relevant LinkedIn and Facebook groups and Google+ communities.

10. Add relevant hashtags when you share your post so more people can find it.

Honestly, Peg does even more than this for her blog posts, but a full account would make your head explode.

6

How to Get More Followers

Do not yearn to be popular; be exquisite.
Do not desire to be famous; be loved.
Do not take pride in being expected;
be palpable, unmistakable.

C. JOYBELL C.

There are only two kinds of people on social media: those who want more followers and those who are lying. A Google search for "how to get more followers" yielded millions of results, which tells you something. This chapter explains how to get more followers, whether you admit you want them or not.

68. Share Good Stuff

Sharing good stuff is 90 percent of the battle of getting more followers. Almost everything else is merely optimization. End of discussion.

69. Jump on New Platforms

Okay, there is one more way to get more followers: jump on a new platform as soon as it opens. It's much easier to amass followers when a platform is new, because there are fewer people to follow and much less noise.

I had 6.4 million followers on Google+ as of July 2014. I jumped on Google+ within weeks of its introduction. If I were to start afresh on Google+ or any other existing platform, I would not be able to catch up to most of the people who started earlier.

Every new platform creates a new set of "stars." For example, I could never catch <u>Joy Cho on Pinterest</u>, where as of July 2014 she had more than 13 million followers. But she would also have difficulty catching me on Google+, where <u>she had only 140 followers at that time</u>. A new platform is a landgrab: if you want to have a lot of followers on it, you have to move rapidly, where "rapidly" means before it's clear that the platform will succeed.

7

How to Socialize Events

I like large parties. They're so intimate.
At small parties there isn't any privacy.

F. SCOTT FITZGERALD, THE GREAT GATSBY

I speak at more than fifty events per year, and I've observed that most organizations do not use social media to increase the visibility and value of events. Instead, they focus on pre-event promotions to drive attendance and do little, if anything, with social media at the event itself.

In 2014, Peg and I staffed the Motorola launch events for the Moto X phone in Mexico, Argentina, Brazil, Peru,

Colombia, and Chile. I was the keynote speaker, and she was the social-media ninja. On this road show, we learned how to rock an event with social media. We're passing our knowledge on to you in this chapter.

70. Pick a Short, Evergreen Hashtag

We could have picked hashtags such as #MotoXBrasil2013, #MotoXMexico2013, or #MotoXPeru2013, but they would have lasted only three days, best case. Instead, we picked a short, generic, evergreen hashtag: #MotoX.

The goal is to choose a hashtag that's trending and constantly in people's faces, whether it refers to an event in Brazil, Mexico, or Peru, or to new television commercials. Uniqueness was a concern with #MotoX, because that term is also used for motocross events. But if I had to choose between short and unique, I would (and did) choose short and deal with the confusion.

71. Integrate the Hashtag into Everything

Use the hashtag from the moment you start promoting the event. That means it's on your website, in all your advertising, and in your e-mail signature. The printed program for the event should have the hashtag on the cover. The introductory slides should publicize it in sixty-point type, and every subsequent slide should have it in the footer. Every employee, speaker, vendor, and guest should know what the hashtag is.

72. Ask Everyone to Use It

It's not enough to tell people the hashtag; you also need to ask them to use it. The conference "voice of God" should ask people to share posts. The event host should do this too. Toward the end of the Moto X tour, I began my keynote addresses with a request that people tweet that they were at the event with the hashtag, and I waited until they did so.

Chutzpah counts on social media.

73. Reach Beyond the Event

The audience for an event is anyone in the world who's interested in your product or service, not only the people at the event. A tweet such as "Not in Brazil? See what Mashable thinks of the #MotoX: http://mashable.com/2013/08/01/moto-x-hands-on/" would be effective, and many people would reshare it.

74. Dedicate a Person

To truly socialize an event, at least one person should focus exclusively on social-media activities. This person will have plenty to do:

- **Before:** Share promotional posts to drive awareness and attendance.

- **During:** Tweet what's happening and take pictures of speakers and guests. Upload these pictures during breaks and reshare other people's posts.

- **After:** Share articles about the event, as well as more pictures and videos. Encourage attendees to reshare their pictures.

<u>Katie Clark</u>, a market researcher, suggests hiring a social-media personality to fill this role if you don't have internal expertise. This person will know what to do, amplify exposure with his or her own accounts, and call in favors from buddies. This is the role Peg filled for Motorola in South America.

75. Stream Live Coverage

Think of how much you're spending to make an event happen. Why wouldn't you broadcast live video coverage? Are you afraid that too many people will place orders? Get real. If you're announcing a product in Bogotá, you want a blogger in Moscow to write about it too.

Don't obsess about the possibility of reducing event attendance. If watching a live stream is as good as attending in person, perhaps the bigger issue is that your event sucks.

76. Provide Real-Time Updates

If you're not live streaming video, have your social-media person provide blow-by-blow updates. Twitter, Instagram, or your blog are probably best for this. Outfits such as The Verge provide <u>outstanding coverage of events such as Apple announcements</u>. You can learn from what they do.

Real-time updates aren't as good as live streaming, but they're cheaper and easier. They're also better for people who cannot watch videos at work because of company policies or low bandwidth.

77. Display the Twitter Stream

Use services that display the tweets containing your hashtag and beam them onto a screen at the conference. Displaying these tweets encourages more interaction and more use of your hashtag. For some people, seeing one of their tweets scroll by is like seeing their picture on the display in Times Square.

Twubs and Tchat are two services that do this and hide retweets in order to eliminate repetition. See related information about displaying tweets in chapter 9 (h/t Bruce Sallan).

78. Provide Wireless Access

Let me get this straight: You're spending thousands of dollars to put on the event. You're pounding your hashtag into everyone and asking them to use it. But you're restricting wireless access. Have you lost your mind?

When you're doing site selection, take a computer or phone and run <u>Speedtest</u> at each facility. Tell the salesperson that you anticipate several hundred people using the network at once, so you'll take your business elsewhere if the facility can't provide good Internet access. If all else fails, bring in mobile hotspots or turn some smartphones into tethering hotspots. There is no excuse for lousy wireless access.

Don't password-protect the network. A password-protected network is the enemy of social-media buzz. If you must password-protect the network, publish the password everywhere—which, of course, means security is an illusion, so you might as well not use a password!

79. Provide a Place to Take Pictures

We set up an area for taking photos at the Moto X events. All that was necessary was good lighting and a backdrop with "Moto X" printed all over it. People saw the backdrop and thought it was "fifteen-minutes of fame" time: *Let's pretend we're Hollywood stars.*

People will share roughly 100 percent of these photos—hopefully with your hashtag.

80. Take and Share Candid Pictures

Hire a professional photographer to take candid pictures at your event. He or she will cost around $1,000 per day, but this is less than you would spend on souvenir USB drives featuring your logo that people don't want.

At the Moto X events, I posed with anyone who asked (and asked anyone who didn't ask me) in front of the backdrop. After each event, we sent an e-mail to guests telling them where they

could find these photos, and we encouraged them to download the pictures and share them with the Moto X hashtag.

81. Put Your Execs to Work

At many events, after company executives speak to the gathering, they rush off to a limited-access press conference or individual interviews. They might make a short public appearance later, during which they're surrounded by their "people" to protect them from who-knows-what. This is a big mistake.

Your executives should go beyond merely being willing to pose for photos with attendees and instead proactively ask people to have a photo taken with them. No one will refuse this request, and roughly 100 percent of those photos will be shared.

82. Cover the Earth

Once you have pictures and video, share them on every platform. We shared photos of the Moto X events on Google+, Twitter, Facebook, and Instagram for Motorola. The goal is to get everyone who was at the event to see the pictures and videos and reshare them. With a little bit of social-media effort and magic, you can make your event look like it was the place to be.

8

How to Run Google+ Hangouts on Air

Reading maketh a full man; conference a ready man;
and writing an exact man.

FRANCIS BACON, "OF STUDIES"

Later in chapter 11 we provide tips for each platform, but we've dedicated this stand-alone chapter to Google+ Hangouts on Air (HOAs) because they are a magical way to rock social media. How else could Desmond Tutu and the Dalai Lama, for example, reach thousands of people in one event?

Even if you're not Desmond Tutu or the Dalai Lama, using Google+ HOAs is like having your own television channel.

Dalai Lama & Desmond Tutu in a Google+ Hangout On Air

This is something you can't do with Facebook, Pinterest, Twitter, or LinkedIn. Here's an <u>HOA about self-publishing</u> to give you an idea of how you can use this Google+ killer app. (This HOA was conducted before Peg and I understood the importance of good lighting!)

An HOA is publicly broadcast through your Google+ page and YouTube channel. Afterward, it is automatically archived to your YouTube channel so that you can share it later. You can start an HOA in just about any country where Google+ is available, <u>with only a few exceptions</u>.

In addition to Hangouts on Air, Google+ offers "regular" Hangouts—video-chat sessions in which up to ten people get together to socialize. These Hangouts are not recorded and are not automatically archived to your YouTube channel. Most of the time they are not worth keeping, much less sharing.

<u>Google+ provides extensive instructions for Hangouts on Air</u>. This chapter offers more power tips for maximizing the success of your HOAs as part of your social-media tool kit.

83. Get the Right Equipment

Hopefully, thousands of people will watch your HOA—some while the event is occurring and many more as a recording. This makes an investment in equipment prudent if not imperative. The total cost of everything you need will be less than $1,000. Here's what I use:

- **Webcam.** The Logitech C920-C webcam is probably a much better camera than the one on your laptop.

- **Microphone and earphones.** The Logitech H530 headset is probably a much better microphone than the one on your laptop.

- **Lighting.** The Westcott uLite 2-Light is probably a much better lighting setup than what's in your office or home. It's certainly better than what Peg and I had when we made the self-publishing HOA mentioned earlier in this chapter. Watch this video by Mari Smith to learn how to light your "studio."

- **Background.** The Fotodiox collapsible background is probably a much better background than all the crap in your home or office will provide.

I sometimes also use a device called SeeEye2Eye. This is a periscope-like device that helps you look at the camera, not people's image on your monitor. This makes viewers think you're looking at them.

You don't really need to buy all this equipment, because most computers offer the same capabilities. However, if you're serious about social media, this would be money well spent.

At the very least, arrange your setup so that your camera is at eye level, look at the camera, and try to remember that whenever you're looking at a person's image, you're not making eye contact with them.

84. Add Structure

There are two theories about structuring HOAs. One theory is that they should be unstructured, spontaneous, and impromptu. This is fine if you're Desmond Tutu or the Dalai Lama.

The other theory is that you should plan, script, and organize your HOAs. We favor this approach in order to maximize the value of each event. Think of yourself as a professor and your HOAs as classes or lectures whose purpose is to inspire viewers to reshare them.

85. Create an Event Page

An event page helps maximize participation by enabling people to add a Google calendar item and an RSVP reminder. Here are <u>instructions for how to do this</u>.

The event page should describe the program and provide links to biographical information about the presenters and time zone information. Adding photos of the speakers to the event page will generate a notification to people who have RSVPed, which is a good reminder to attend the event.

86. Create a Custom Header

A custom header for your event page will increase its visibility. Ronnie Bincer, the guy behind The Hangout Helper website, <u>explains how here</u>. The header should be 300 by 1200 pixels. This is an example of a custom header:

87. Create a Trailer

A video trailer is an excellent way to promote your HOA. A trailer is something for your speakers and followers to share to get more people to show up. Jeff Sieh, creator of The Manly Show, is a master at making trailers; he <u>explains how here</u>. Invest forty-one seconds and watch his trailer.

88. Create a Lower-Third Custom Overlay

A lower-third custom overlay is a label that contains your name and affiliation and runs in the lower third of your video. It's a little touch that makes an HOA look more professional. You can create one with the Hangout Toolbox or by using the <u>HangoutMagix</u> website.

89. Invite Your Speakers Via E-mail

When you start your HOA, you can invite your speakers via a +mention or an e-mail. We recommend doing both, because speakers who get many +mention notifications will have trouble finding the one for your event. Also, some of your speakers may not even know where to look for notifications.

Tell your speakers to keep the link in the invitation handy so that if they are booted out of the HOA or leave accidentally, they can get right back in. This happens to me at least once during every HOA, so keep the link handy for yourself too.

90. Enable People to Watch in More Places

People don't have to be Google+ members to watch an HOA. If you embed code or the YouTube URL in your blog or website, people can see the HOA live or watch the recording later.

A service called 22Social enables people to watch an HOA on Facebook. By using this service, you can cross-promote and broadcast your HOA on your Facebook Page as well.

Mari Smith uses this technique with great success. She's great on camera, so she can gain more followers on Google+ by letting her Facebook fans see her live and "in person" on

HOAs. Facebook followers can find a 22Social event via a tab or a link that can be shared on any platform.

91. Wear Solid Colors

Video cameras do strange things to clothes that contain complex patterns and stripes. The effect is called "moiré," and it looks like waviness in the video. The way to prevent this is to wear clothes without patterns and to stick to solid colors.

Photo credit: Eric Harvey Brown.

92. Send a Checklist

Peg and I once did an HOA with an author who, five minutes before it was scheduled to start, told us he didn't have a Google+ account. This was after we had sent several e-mails to him asking if he had an account and requesting that he run test HOAs. People don't know what they don't know, and they don't always ask.

Send the following checklist to your speakers (minus the stuff in parentheses) to help them get their act together. A little bit of preparation will save a lot of aggravation later.

- Do you have a Google+ account? (The number of speakers who agree to do a Hangout but who aren't on Google+ might surprise you.)

- Do you know your Google password? (The number of people who do not might surprise you too.)

- Do you have adequate lighting to illuminate your face from the front?

- Do you have a microphone or headset? A built-in microphone and speakers are insufficient.

- Does your computer have a built-in webcam? (The number of people who don't have a webcam might surprise you.)

- Have you installed the Google+ HOA app? (The first

time someone participates in an HOA, he or she must install an app.)

- Have you arranged not to be interrupted except by cute pets and kids?

- Is your location quiet?

- Are the ringers on your phones turned off?

- Have you promoted the HOA to your followers and through your e-mail database?

- Have you provided your cell-phone number to the host and asked for his or her cell-phone number?

93. Rehearse and Start Early

If you wanted to create a confusing and convoluted user interface, you could use the HOA design as an aspirational goal. You could then compound the problem by changing the user interface the day after people have finally figured it out like Google does.

Every HOA I've participated in has had moments like the following scenario. Seriously. I'm not kidding about the questions you'll encounter.

"Joe, we can't hear you. You're probably muted."
"How do I unmute myself?"

*"See that microphone in the middle of the menu bar
on the top of the window?"*

"No, I don't see anything like that."

"Try clicking on the window."

"I'm in an office. There aren't any windows here."

"Look in the chat area for my instructions."

"What chat area?"

*"Click on the blue thing in the top left corner of the
window."*

*"I told you, I'm in an office. There are no windows
here."*

You need to conduct a full rehearsal and to start at least thirty minutes early, because the HOA interface will perplex 100 percent of your guests 100 percent of the time.

9

How to Rock a
Twitter Chat

*Sometimes when it looks like I'm deep in thought
I'm just trying not to have a conversation with people.*

PETE WENTZ

A Twitter chat is a live event in which people include a
hashtag in their tweets to discuss a topic. A host tweets
questions with the hashtag, and a guest tweets responses
with the same hashtag. Audience members search for the
hashtag to see the discussion and chime in with questions,
comments, and retweets.

Twitter chats present a special challenge because guests

need to think and type rapidly. By contrast, Google+ Hangouts on Air require you to think and *speak* rapidly. Most people find it easier to think and speak than to think and type. This chapter will help you rock Twitter chats as a guest or a host.

94. Use the Right Tools

Twitter chats present two challenges: first, remembering to include the chat's hashtag in every tweet; and second, coping

with the furious flow of tweets. For these reasons, I recommend two tools, Tchat and Twubs, because both automatically include the hashtag in your tweets and also hide retweets.
These are the same tools I mentioned for displaying tweets
during events in chapter 7.

With Tchat and Twubs, you don't have to remember to
type or paste in the hashtag, and you won't see everyone's
retweets during the chat. Hiding the retweets will signifi-
cantly reduce the number of tweets in your stream, which
will make it much easier to follow along.

Peg likes to use TweetDeck for Twitter chats, with three
columns: (1) @mentions, (2) a search for the hashtag, and
(3) direct messages.

Prior to being a host or a guest on a Twitter chat, test
the different methods and see which one works best for you.

95. Pick a Short, Evergreen Hashtag

A short, unique hashtag is easier to remember, requires less
typing for the people who don't use tools such as Tchat and
Twubs, and leaves more characters for the actual tweets. (Remember, Twitter has a 140-character limit.) This is the same
concept as using the hashtag for socializing an event, dis-
cussed in chapter 7.

An evergreen hashtag increases brand awareness once

the chat is over and is useful if your chat becomes a regular event. You don't want to have to retrain people to use a new hashtag. Pick something short, easy to spell, and easy to remember. For example, we use #Canva for any Twitter chat about Canva.

96. Prepare Your Guests

A Twitter chat is one of the most chaotic experiences on social media. Dozens of people might be asking you and your guests questions and making comments at the same time. As a host, you need to prepare yourself and your guests for this chaos, because few people have ever encountered such an intense level of interaction. Here are three suggestions:

- **Be audience driven.** A Twitter chat is not necessarily about what you or your guests want to promote, but about what the audience wants to discuss. Thus your guests need to react rapidly, succinctly, and truthfully, and resist the temptation to overly promote an agenda.

- **Stay Q&A-centered.** Answering as many questions as possible is critical for the success of a Twitter chat. The key is to focus on finding the tweets that have a question mark in them. Ignore any that are irrelevant, repetitious, or stupid, and don't worry about addressing every comment and question, because no one can tell that you haven't.

- **Draft in advance.** Send your guests a list of likely questions before the chat so that they can review them. This will give them the opportunity to prepare responses, gather resources they might want to share, and draft answers to make rapid responses easier. The ability to fake spontaneity is a powerful advantage in a Twitter chat.

97. Type Fast

Speed is everything in a Twitter chat, so if you're a slow typist, you're hosed. I don't expect you to practice your typing with <u>Mavis Beacon</u>, but you should recruit a great typist to enter your responses. Note that the typist's job is to type what you say, not to edit, advise, or ensure that what you tweet isn't boring.

The faster you or your surrogate can type, the more you can respond, and the more you can respond, the more successful the Twitter chat will be. In fact, you might want to practice typing 140-character messages. The goal is to entertain, interest, and inform in fewer than 140 characters and less than thirty seconds.

98. @mention Your Responses

When you respond to a question or comment, be sure to @mention the person. This means that you type "@" and the person's screen name. The recipient and the audience can then see that your tweet is directed toward a specific person's question or comment.

99. Spread the Word

If you're asked to be a guest on someone else's Twitter chat, spread the word. Doing so will help the host by bringing new guests to his or her chat and also give your followers the opportunity to come and tweet with you.

100. Summarize

After the Twitter chat is over, gather all the tweets, remove the retweets and comments, and provide a summary. Here's an <u>example of a Twitter chat</u> that we hosted for *APE: Author, Publisher, Entrepreneur—How to Publish a Book* during the book launch, using a service called <u>Storify</u> to organize the summary.

The summary should contain the best questions and their

answers. You can add content from Amazon, Instagram, Facebook, and YouTube to make it more interesting. This is an excellent way to give a chat a longer life. Once you have the summary, send it to attendees and registrants, and share it everywhere you can.

10

How to Avoid Looking Clueless

The whole problem with the world is that fools and
fanatics are always so certain of themselves,
but wiser people so full of doubts.

BERTRAND RUSSELL

Take this quick test:

- Does the pronunciation of Steve Jobs's last name rhyme with *robes* or *robs*?

- Is the pronunciation of Lucchese, the Texas boot company, "Lu-cheese-ee" or "Lu-kay-zee"?

- Is the pronunciation of *quay*, as in Sydney, Australia's Circular Quay, "kway" or "key"?

The right answer for each is the second choice. When people make the wrong choices, they look clueless to insiders. We don't want you to look clueless on social media, so read on to get clued in.

101. Don't Be an Orifice

In the words of Thumper's father in the movie *Bambi*, "If you can't say somethin' nice, don't say nothin' at all." Edification is great. Sarcasm is great. Belligerence is lame. Denigration of other points of view is lame. Complaining that a post is not perfect for you is lame. If you don't like a post, shut up and move on.

102. Don't Tell People What to Share

Telling people what to share is not just a sign of cluelessness, it's a *billboard* of cluelessness. If you don't like what a person shares, don't follow him or her. You're not paying to read the person's post, so don't feel entitled to tell him or her what to share. The sun doesn't revolve around the earth, and the Internet doesn't revolve around you.

103. Don't Buy Followers, Likes, or +1s

Only losers and charlatans buy followers, likes, and +1s. (Can we tell you how we really feel?) I don't deny that people think that a large number of followers is social proof of goodness, but buying followers is cheating. Here's how large companies slide down the slippery slope.

- The CEO attends a conference or reads *Fast Company* and decides that her company has to use social media more.

- She tells the chief marketing officer (CMO) that she wants to see some results, where results mean an increase in the number of followers, likes, and +1s.

- The CMO realizes there's no one who understands social media in the company (which is probably not true, but I digress), so the easy, safe, and seemingly logical choice is to hire someone from one of the company's agencies, since these agencies are full of experts.

- The first thing the social-media hire does is retain his former agency to achieve the CMO's objectives.

- The agency asks for and receives a large budget that includes enough money to buy followers, likes, and +1s to achieve the stated objectives.

- The agency spends the budget and, big surprise, achieves the numbers. Victory is declared, and everyone is happy.

Meanwhile, because the followers, likes, and +1s are not "real," social media fails to deliver meaningful results. Purchased followers, likes, and +1s provide no lasting benefits, since they don't interact with your content and have no interest in your posts. You may never be caught buying your way into social media, but to do so is pissing on your karma, and karma is a bitch.

There is one exception to our distaste for buying your way in, and that's paying to promote Facebook posts or Pages. This is simply the way Facebook works—it's the same as buying advertising on other media. However, that's where we draw the line.

104. Don't Ask People to Follow You

If you want more followers, earn them with the quality of your posts. If Groucho Marx were alive today, he'd amend his famous joke and say that people who ask you to follow them aren't worth following. Maintain your dignity, don't grovel for followers, and share good stuff in large quantities.

Don't confuse asking people to follow you with adding

social links on your blog. Social links are a subtle invitation to follow you, which is not the same as tweeting "Please follow me."

105. Don't Ask People to Reshare Your Posts

If your posts are good, this will happen naturally. If you employ all the techniques we've explained, people will read your posts. If they're good, people will reshare them. It's that simple. The only time it's acceptable to ask for reshares is when a post is philanthropic in nature.

106. Don't Announce Your Unfollows

No one cares if you stopped following someone. This is equivalent to standing up in the middle-school cafeteria and announcing that you're no longer someone's friend. Few people will unfollow someone just because you did, so get over yourself.

107. Don't Ask Why People Unfollowed You

Changing the mix of those you follow is a continuing process, so don't panic when people unfollow you. If you ask why, you may lose even more followers by raising doubt: *Maybe I should unfollow him or her too*. At the very least, people may take you less seriously. Instead, keep sharing, commenting, and responding, and don't stress over those who leave.

108. Don't Be a Pimp

Social media is a great way to promote your product, service, or website—that's why we're making all this effort. You'll look clueless, however, if more than one out of twenty of your posts are promotional. Imagine if NPR ran pledge drives every day.

109. Don't Swear

Swearing is bullshit. (I've waited a long time to write something that clever.) Somewhere along the way, swearing on social media became a sign of openness, sincerity, and authenticity. Go figure. Profanity is a sign that you're inarticulate, if not clueless, so rarely use it unless, for example, you want to make a strong statement about SEO.

110. Don't Call Yourself a Guru or an Expert

If you are a guru or an expert, people will know it. If you aren't one, no one is going to believe you. In particular, "social-media guru" is an oxymoron because nobody really knows how social media works—including Peg and me!

No matter how smart you are, best practices always change, because the platforms change how their sites work. Therefore, everyone needs to keep experimenting. Also, we've noticed that the folks who are least likely to conduct experiments are the self-declared experts who think they know everything.

111. Don't Abdicate to an Agency

If you hire a digital agency that puts ten people in a "war room" to "measure sentiment" along your "brand ethos" and then needs forty-five days to compose a tweet, this book has failed you.

Do not abdicate your social media to "experts" who have a hundred followers, tweet once a month, and charge you more than the GNP of a small nation for their services. A good rule of thumb is never to take the advice of someone who has fewer followers than you.

If you practice what we preach, you won't need an agency.

If you practice what we preach and you *are* an agency, perhaps you can now justify your rates.

112. Don't Delegate Your Social Media to an Intern

The fact that you found a young person who uses Facebook and will work for a hourly wage lower than a fast-food employee's doesn't mean that you should hire him or her to manage your social media. This is like believing that having a penis makes a person a urologist or owning a car makes a person a mechanic.

Don't get us wrong; we love interns. They bring fresh perspectives and sensibilities to social media. We just want to ensure that you take social media seriously and put qualified people on it. At least require your interns to read this book, and then monitor every post and comment they make for a few weeks.

11

How to Optimize for Individual Platforms

The five Ps of social media: Google+ is for passions;
Facebook is for people; LinkedIn is for pimping;
Pinterest is for pictures; Twitter is for perception.
Let's see Philip Kotler top this.

GUY KAWASAKI

We love travel guides to cities that highlight must-see places and must-do activities, so we're going to use that technique to provide tips and tricks for each platform. Like cities, platforms have nuances, best practices, and modus operandi. The purpose of this chapter is to help you optimize your experience for each platform.

113. Tips for Facebook

Grok EdgeRank

Not all of the people who follow you on Facebook see everything that you share in their <u>News Feed</u>. The theory is that Facebook doesn't want people swamped by posts, so it uses indicators such as the number of comments, the kind of story, and black magic to decide which of your followers can see your posts. Facebook calls this concept "EdgeRank," and it's supposed to motivate you to strive for more interaction so that more people see what you share.

On my soapbox: I dislike that Facebook works this way because I believe that people who voluntarily follow you should see everything you share. If you share too much or share what they don't like, it's easy enough for them to unfollow you.

Use Facebook's Page Insights

Facebook's <u>Page Insights</u> provides statistics to help you determine what's working for your account. You can use this data for targeting your sponsored posts, finding out what posts are popular, and understanding the demographics of your followers.

Link Your Instagram Account to Your Facebook Page

You can <u>link your Instagram account to your Facebook Page</u>. This means that when you share a photo on Instagram, it will automatically appear on your Facebook Page. Just remember that you did this so that you don't inadvertently share an Instagram photo that you don't want everyone on Facebook to see.

Embed Videos

There's good news and bad news when it comes to embedded videos on Facebook. The bad news is that they appear in a small window. The good news is that they automatically play in people's News Feed, making them more eye-catching. Both things considered, embedded videos are a good way to add drama to your Facebook posts.

Interact with Other Facebook Pages

Our Facebook buddies told us they think managers of Pages should share and comment on other Pages. This is supposed to increase how often your Page is displayed. We don't know whether this is true or how much it matters, but it can't hurt to try.

Experiment

More than any other platform, we cannot figure out how to optimize Facebook posts. For example, our goal is that every post contain a big graphic whether people read it on a computer, Android device, or iOS device, and as far as we can tell, this is impossible. We recommend that you keep experimenting because no one, except for maybe Mark Zuckerberg, knows what Facebook wants.

114. Tips for Google+

Think Twice About Starting a Community

<u>Google+ communities</u> are great places to find people who share your passions or to learn about new topics. Although it's great to join a community, think long and hard about starting a community, because you will be managing it for a long time.

I've started several communities and don't want to manage them anymore. A public community runs itself, but a private community needs someone to approve people who want to join it.

Peg's analogy is that starting a community is like getting a puppy: it sounds like a good idea in the beginning, but you have to clean up after it and train it. Also, when it grows up, it may no longer be cute.

Check How Google+ Reads Your Posts

Did you know that Google+ will autofill a hashtag? Share a few Google+ posts that include two of your best guesses at hashtags. Then look at what Google+ adds as the third

hashtag. If Google+'s additions are way off, you need to alter your content creation and curation. For example, if you're trying to reach designers but Google+ thinks your content is about travel, you've got a problem (h/t <u>Yifat Cohen</u>).

Get Your Name in the News

<u>Google News</u> curates news from around the world. The most popular stories display a button that says "See realtime coverage." Click on this button, and to the right of the story you can enter a Google+ comment. Other people will see your

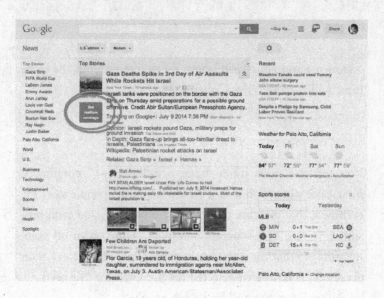

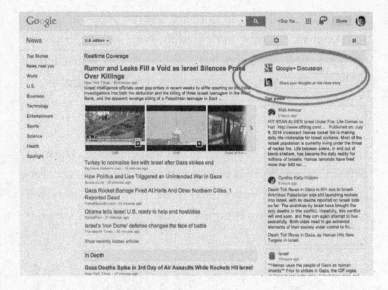

comment, and your visibility to those interested in the same topic will rise (h/t Yifat Cohen).

Use Comments and +1s to Run Polls

You can run polls by enabling people to "+1" comments. First, pose a question with a post and instruct people to +1 the comment that matches their response. Second, add each possible response as a separate comment. Third, turn off commenting, so that the only action people can take is to +1 their choice. This is how we selected the final title for this book.

Note: Even our poll had a big graphic!

Use Ripples to Find the Best Resharers

Google+'s <u>Ripples</u> feature shows the activity of public posts by displaying who has publicly reshared your posts. This information can help you determine whom you should thank and follow. Plus, it's a cool graphic to look at.

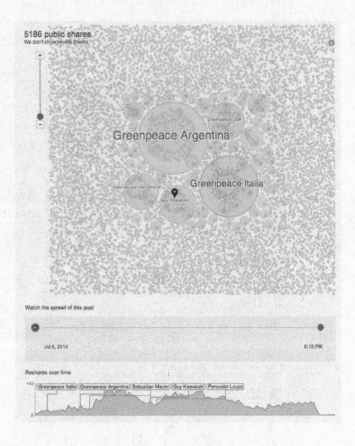

Use Replies and More

<u>Replies and More</u> is the most valuable Google+ extension in the world, and I am amazed that Google hasn't added its functionality into Google+. It enables you to reply to someone and trigger a notification to him or her without having

to type "@" and the person's name. This procedure increases the likelihood of a response.

Add a Google+ Profile Badge to Your Website

You can <u>embed your Google+ profile badge</u> in your blog or website to facilitate people reading your Google+ page. Learn more about <u>optimizing this badge here</u> (h/t <u>Susana Morin</u>). Alternatively, you can <u>add a Google+ Follow button</u> if you'd like to use less space on your page.

Stylize Your Text

Google+ enables you to stylize text in a post for a bit more drama.

- **Bold.** Asterisk on each side: *your text*
- *Italics.* Underscore on each side: _your text_
- ~~Strikethrough.~~ Hyphen on each side: -your text-

You can make this easier by using the <u>Chrome extension called Post Editor</u>. This provides formatting options in a composer box.

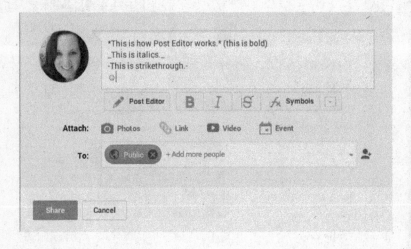

You can also add characters to your posts by using <u>Copy Paste Character</u> to grab special characters such as and ❄.

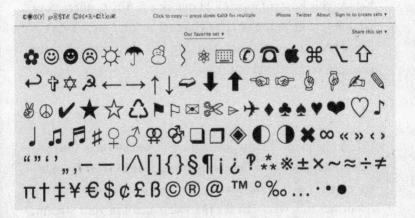

Use the Hashtag of the Day

You can piggyback on the Google+ community's "hashtags of the day." For example, if you share a story about science on Sunday, many people are likely to read it because they subscribe to <u>#ScienceSunday</u>. There are many hashtags of the day, such as <u>#Caturday</u>, <u>#StarWarsTuesday</u>, and <u>#Word-lessWednesday</u>.

Connect Your Google+ Page to Your YouTube Channel

Before you host a Google+ Hangout on Air, connect your Google+ page and YouTube channel so that your HOA is broadcast and archived. You can do this through your <u>Google+</u> or <u>YouTube settings</u>.

Comment on YouTube Videos

When members of Google+ make a comment on a YouTube video, the video and the comment appear in their Google+ streams. This is good for the creator of the video because his or her followers can see the video again in your stream, and it's good for you because it adds content to your stream.

115. Tips for Instagram

Keep It Simple

You can only share pictures on Instagram and only from mobile phones and tablets, so don't overthink what you do on it. Take interesting—mostly slice-of-life—photos, add a five- to ten-word witty caption, add two or three hashtags, and share. Boom, this is your Instagram strategy!

Piggyback on Popular Hashtags

Hashtags go crazy on Instagram. Some popular hashtags you can jump on are #instagood, #instatravel, and #latergram (for posting an older photo). You should add two or three relevant hashtags to your posts.

Unlike other platforms, you can get away with adding more hashtags in a comment for more visibility. (You'd look clueless if you did this elsewhere.) You can find the most popular hashtags by using Iconosquare. A great time saver is to save groups of hashtags in Evernote to cut and paste into Instagram.

TagsForLikes and Instatag are phone apps that help you find lists of popular hashtags that you can cut and paste into the comments of your Instagram post. Populagram is a website that posts popular hashtags, users, locations, and filters.

Finesse the Filters

The most popular Instagram filters are Normal, Valencia, Earlybird, and X-Pro II. (You can check what's popular here.) Sticking with these is a safe bet. For a custom look, you can use more than one app to process your photos. For example, use Camera+ to take the photo and filter it, then use a secondary filter in Instagram.

At the other end of the spectrum, #NoFilter is one of the most popular hashtags on Instagram.

No matter what your filter strategy is, make sure that people realize the effects are intentional—as opposed to their thinking you're sharing a lousy photo.

Don't Show Off

The universe can tolerate only a limited number of selfies and food and travel photos, so avoid making your Instagram account into a bragfest. The correct subliminal message is *Share this moment with me*, not *Look at me, I'm so cool.* Use your photos to tell visual stories, and don't oversell yourself.

Share Your Instagram Photos on Twitter

In addition to sharing Instagram posts on Facebook, you can share Instagram posts on Twitter. A service called If This Then That (<u>IFTTT</u>) connects social-media platforms by triggering such an action. A sample IFTTT "recipe" follows. Remember, if you do this, every Instagram photo will get tweeted.

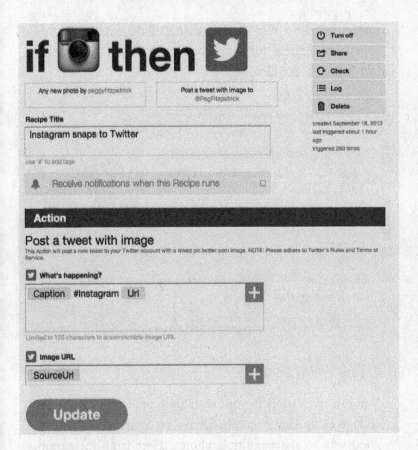

Add an Instagram Widget to Your Blog or Website

You can add an Instagram widget to your blog or website to show your latest masterpieces, encourage Instagram activity, and gain new followers. There are widgets to create image sliders for WordPress, photo grid displays for Word-Press, and galleys for non-WordPress blogs and websites (h/t Marty McPadden).

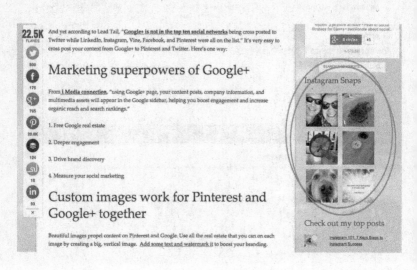

Create Photo Collages

You can add variety to your Instagram photos by creating a collage using Color Splash, Diptic, or Snapseed. This is a good way to share multiple photos. Here is an Instagram collage created by Calvin Lee, the brand strategist of Mayhem Studios, at the Los Angeles Auto Show:

Use Instagram Reposting Apps

You can reshare other people's Instagram photos with <u>Repost for Instagram</u> and <u>Photo Repost</u>. These apps are a great way for brands to showcase their customers' Instagram photos.

116. Tips for LinkedIn

Write a Personalized Connection Request

A few years ago, LinkedIn told me that I had the most pending connection requests of any user. I usually ignore these requests because few are personalized. Instead, they often start with "I'd like to add you to my professional network on LinkedIn," which is the default message in the outgoing e-mail.

If you want LinkedIn to work as a way to make connections, you need to personalize your requests. Be aware that when you send mobile connection requests, you don't get the option to customize them, so this task is best done on your computer.

Get Serious

The serious and professional nature of LinkedIn means that you should not share quotes or popular memes such as cat photos. You should assume that a potential employer or business partner will check your LinkedIn posts someday. I don't want to be a killjoy, but you also should seldom share a post on LinkedIn containing a YouTube video with the intent of entertaining people.

Focus on a Niche

On LinkedIn, more so than on other platforms, it's a good idea to stay focused on a few core topics to establish thought leadership. I share content on innovation, entrepreneurship, writing, and technology. Peg shares content on social media, marketing, and writing. We both share other relevant articles that we like, but our focus is on our niches.

Participate in Groups

Groups are a great way to meet people in your industry and discuss career-related topics. You can choose to receive e-mail notifications for conversations that you're taking part in.

Add Video Interviews and Google+ HOAs

Make sure to keep your profile current and impressive by adding links to your video interviews and Hangouts on Air. When you get in the flow of doing these things, you might forget to deploy them to LinkedIn.

Share Your SlideShare Presentations

Share your SlideShare presentations as a short-form LinkedIn update and also embed them in long-form published posts.

117. Tips for Pinterest

Don't Pin Your Personal Photos

Pinterest isn't the place to share pictures you took yourself unless you're a fantastic photographer like Trey Ratcliff, own an amazing car collection like <u>Jay Leno</u>, or you are a food or fashion blogger with fantastic photos. In other words, for most people Pinterest isn't Instagram.

Add Pinterest Goodies

Pinterest offers these goodies to enhance the Pinterest experience for you and your readers:

- Pinterest for iOS, so that you can view and pin from your Apple device

- Pinterest for Android, so that you can view and pin from your Android device

- A "Pin it" button to help people pin things from your website or blog

- A pin widget to embed one of your pins in your website or blog

- A widget to embed a frame with up to thirty of your latest pins in your website or blog

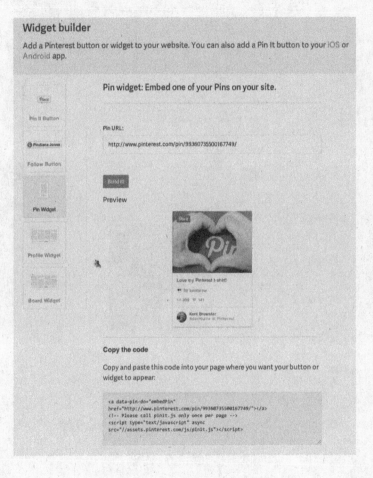

Widget builder

Add a Pinterest button or widget to your website. You can also add a Pin It button to your iOS or Android app.

Pin widget: Embed one of your Pins on your site.

Pin It Button

Pindiana Jones

Follow Button

Pin Widget

Profile Widget

Board Widget

Pin URL:

http://www.pinterest.com/pin/99360735500167749/

Build it

Preview

Love my Pinterest t-shirt!

Kent Brewster

Copy the code

Copy and paste this code into your page where you want your button or widget to appear:

```
<a data-pin-do="embedPin"
href="http://www.pinterest.com/pin/99360735500167749/"></a>
<!-- Please call pinit.js only once per page -->
<script type="text/javascript" async
src="//assets.pinterest.com/js/pinit.js"></script>
```

Widget builder

Add a Pinterest button or widget to your website. You can also add a Pin It button to your iOS or Android app.

Post

Pin It Button

Pindiana Jones

Follow Button

Pin Widget

Profile Widget

Board Widget

Profile widget: Show up to 30 of your latest Pins on your site.

Pinterest User URL:

http://www.pinterest.com/pinterest/

Custom Sizes: Square   Sidebar   Header   Roll Your Own

Build It

Preview

Copy the code

Copy and paste this code into your page where you want your button or widget to appear:

```
<a data-pin-do="embedUser" href="http://www.pinterest.com/pinterest/" data-
pin-scale-width="80" data-pin-scale-height="320" data-pin-board-width="400">
</a>
<!-- Please call pinit.js only once per page -->
<script type="text/javascript" async
src="//assets.pinterest.com/js/pinit.js"></script>
```

Use Secret Boards

You can collaborate with others on private projects via secret boards. You can also build boards over time, keeping them secret and then releasing them when you're done.

If you're creating a Pinterest campaign, keep in mind that you need to work backward. The pin that you want to appear as the first pin (in the upper left corner) should be the last one you add.

Start Collaborative Boards

With collaborative boards, you can reach other people's Pinterest followers and have multiple pinners adding content. Group boards are rich resources that help other pinners and also help you by providing you with great pins.

Rotate Your Pinterest Boards

Put the most popular board at the top to show how interesting you are. Move holiday or themed boards to the top to highlight them. Using Tailwind, a third-party Pinterest app, you can find out which boards are currently the most popular and pay special attention to them.

Rotate Pinning on Boards

You want to have a pin on each board, not all the pins on one board, and a pin on a range of boards so that people checking your Pinterest stream will see a variety of pins. The "eye candy" nature of Pinterest demands a steady stream of beautiful pins.

Add Categories and Descriptions

Each board title and description should include keywords that will help people find you through Guided Search. Tell people what the board is about so they can decide whether they'd like to follow it.

Share Your Pins on Other Social Networks

Tweet your pins and add links to pins when you share content on other social platforms. If people like a pin enough to share it, they might want to save it to a Pinterest board of their own.

Stick with It

Don't start a board and abandon it after one pin. Boards with fewer than ten pins are ineffective. If you start a new board, keep your focus on it for a few weeks and pin to it regularly.

Update Your Cover Photos

Keep your Pinterest page fresh by changing the covers on your boards. Aim to create an overall visual message that will interest other pinners.

118. Tips for SlideShare

Differentiate Between SlideShare and PowerPoint

SlideShare doesn't provide audio, so people must understand your message from the slides alone. By contrast, a person usually *presents* PowerPoint slides, adding to the message with his or her oral presentation. Thus, merely taking your PowerPoint slides and uploading them to SlideShare is risky, because PowerPoint slides should contain a minimal amount of text, according to at least one expert.

Whereas the <u>optimal format for PowerPoint is slides with minimal text</u> accompanied by an oral explanation, the optimal format for SlideShare is slides with self-explanatory text, because that is the only explanation most SlideShare users will ever see.

Create a Compelling Title Page

Another difference between SlideShare and PowerPoint is that a SlideShare presentation requires a much better title page than a PowerPoint presentation. Whereas hardly anyone pays attention to the title page of a PowerPoint presentation, because all eyes are on the presenter, the title page of a SlideShare presentation must inspire people to click through.

Repurpose Your Past Successes

You can extend the life of your most popular blog posts by turning them into SlideShare presentations. Peg has taken blog posts that I shared months earlier and made them successful on SlideShare. For example, I wrote a blog post called "The Art of Branding" that she turned into a SlideShare presentation viewed by seventy thousand people.

Cover the Basics

When you upload a SlideShare presentation, make sure you provide all of the following information:

- **Title.** This is the name of your presentation. It should include descriptive keywords to attract viewers. Example: "Let's Stop the Glorification of Busy."

- **Description.** This is a short summary that tells the story of your presentation, such as how it was originally presented and for what purpose. You can use up to three thousand characters. Example: "I published a blog post about the takeaways that I derived from reading Arianna Huffington's book *Thrive: The Third Metric to Redefining Success and Creating a Life of Well-Being, Wisdom, and Wonder.* This presentation is a summary of that blog post and why we should add 'thriving' as a metric for success in life."

- **Category.** This is the broad category or type of subject matter of your presentation. There are approximately forty choices such as design, business, education, and technology. SlideShare uses these categories to organize presentations into logical groups.

- **Tags.** These are terms that will help people find your presentation when they search SlideShare. Examples: "Arianna Huffington, business"; "Guy Kawasaki, leadership, success, third metric, thrive, balance, work, life, family." You can add up to twenty tags to your SlideShare presentation. Using tags increases visibility by 30 percent, according to SlideShare.

Include a Call to Action (CTA)

You can use your last slide in a SlideShare presentation to provide clickable links to other SlideShare presentations, your blog, or an invitation to follow you on SlideShare or other social-media platforms.

Share Your Masterpiece

Embedded SlideShare presentations look great on Twitter, Pinterest, and LinkedIn, but not on Google+ and Facebook. When I share a SlideShare presentation on the last two platforms, I take a screen capture of the title page and provide a link rather than embed the presentation itself.

119. Tips for Twitter

Add a Graphic to Your Tweets

A graphic is worth a thousand characters. Which tweets do you think attract more attention: the ones with or without graphics?

You can add up to four pictures to a tweet, which is sweet.

Tweets

Guy Kawasaki @GuyKawasaki · now
My day at Madame Tussauds in Sydney pic.twitter.com/Bk39NGlqLM

View photo

Jesus Alvarez @alvarezval · 24s
Ecommece: la multicanalidad para una atención al cliente más cercana
wp.me/p31CXU-LJ

Ivan @ivan2266 · 25s
ift.tt/1IXVJEN via /r/pics ift.tt/1mP9ZFP Lightning Ridge Black Opal
fb.me/3hTSWAv54

Stefanie Fauquet @MommyMusings · 25s
National Geographic photo du jour: ift.tt/n1qxxR #travel #photography NatGeo
pic.twitter.com/Oy90SeQCiz

View photo

To do this, click the camera icon repeatedly.

Tag People in Your Photos

You can tag up to ten people per photo, and the tag doesn't affect the character count of your tweet. The people who are tagged will receive a notification, and this may increase engagement.

Lanae
@SocialNetNanny

Love the new Facebook cover photo I just
designed with @canva! Easy to use,
perfectly size layouts, clean & crisp.

10:58 AM - 12 Jun 2014

Flag media

Repeat Your Tweets

In chapter 3, I explained how repeating my tweets four times
increases clicks by a factor of four or more. But this advice
is so contrary to what most experts say that I wanted to repeat it in case you missed it the first time—which illustrates
the point of repeating tweets.

Master Addressing

You have to see the movie <u>Chef</u> if you're interested in social media, and you must be interested in social media if you're reading this book. In the movie, the chef (@ChefCarlCasper) supposedly makes a rookie mistake by berating a restaurant critic (@RamseyMichel) with this tweet: "@RamseyMichel You wouldn't know a good meal if it sat on your face" (h/t <u>Frank Sugino</u>).

The tweet goes viral and leads first to a confrontation with the restaurant's owner and then to the chef's firing. The movie is inaccurate, however, because only people who were following both the chef and the critic would have seen the tweet, and the chef created his account immediately before he created the tweet, so he would not have had any followers. Therefore, no one would have seen the tweet unless the critic retweeted it.

Slight poetic license aside, there's an important lesson here: Master addressing tweets. For example, suppose @LoserCEO tweets, "@GuyKawasaki I photocopied *Art of the Start* for my team. Am I scrappy or an asshole?" This table explains who can see my response, depending on how I address it.

MY TWEET	WHO CAN SEE IT
"@LoserCEO You are a scrappy asshole."	Initially, only @LoserCEO and people who follow both of us will see it. If someone who follows both of us retweets my response, it can spread.
".@LoserCEO You are a scrappy asshole." (Note the dot in front of "@LoserCEO")	Anyone who follows me can see it, and they should intuit that this is a response to @LoserCEO that I mean for everyone to see.
"You are a scrappy asshole."	Anyone who follows me can see it, but there's no way for them to know this was meant as a response specifically to @LoserCEO. People might interpret this as my telling all my followers that they are scrappy assholes.

Remember that when you address a tweet with @name, only you, the recipient, and people who follow you both can see the tweet. If you want the world to see your tweet, add at least a dot in front of the name—for example, ".@GuyKawasaki I love your books."

Activate Notifications

You can <u>activate notifications</u> on Twitter so that you receive an e-mail when important things happen, such as when your tweets are retweeted or when new people follow you. This will help you somewhat tame the river of information that flows through Twitter (h/t Ryan Mobilia).

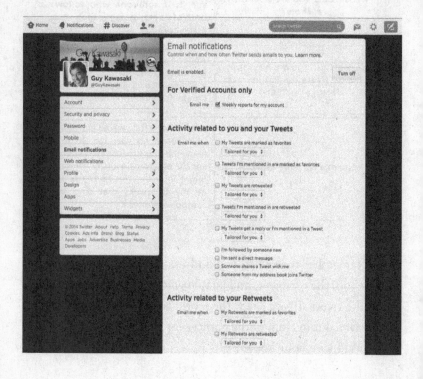

Twitter cards provide a richer media appearance for your tweets. All you have to do is add a few lines of HTML code to your blog or website. Then when people tweet links to your blog or website, a card is attached to the tweet that is visible to all their followers. This card can contain up to four photos, a link to a mobile app, video or audio media, or product information. Twitter cards also provide analytics to help you improve the performance of your tweets.

120. Tips for YouTube

Complete Your Profile in the "About" Section

Complete your YouTube profile to help convince people to watch your videos. Include keywords and what your posting schedule is so that people know what to expect. Be sure to add links to your website and social-media accounts too (h/t <u>Tara Ross</u>).

Create a Channel Trailer

A channel trailer is a short advertising spot for your channel. It acts as a standard "welcome" when people visit your channel's home page. You can learn <u>how to add one here</u>. Watch <u>Jeff Sieh's</u> for some inspiration.

Create an Intro and Outro

An intro and outro is a short clip (three to four seconds) with a jingle and your picture or logo. Watch this <u>Marques Brownlee video</u> to see what we mean. These short pieces will add a lot to the professionalism of your videos.

Organize Your Content

Channel sections allow you to customize, organize, and promote your YouTube channel. Go to your channel home tab and click on "Add a section" to do this.

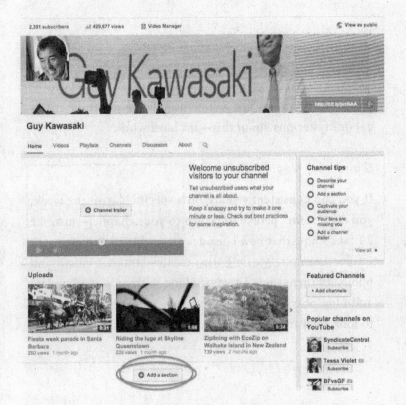

Add Keywords and Descriptions for Each Video

Add keywords and clear descriptions so that people can find your videos via a search. Include the names of the people in the videos, and make sure that your videos are in the proper categories.

Respond to Comments

Perhaps more than on any other platform, you should respond to comments on YouTube. Responding is how popular people build their YouTube followings. There's nothing magical or mysterious about this—it's hard work.

Share on a Regular Schedule

If you can consistently share on a specific day of the week, you can "train" people to return to your channel—just like 24 fans know that new episodes air on Monday nights.

For example, Marie Forleo creates fantastic videos and publishes them each Tuesday, along with an e-mail update and blog post for each. This gives her followers something to look forward to each week.

12

How to Put Everything Together

Time you enjoy wasting is not wasted time.

MARTHE TROLY-CURTIN

T his chapter is a case study of how to put everything together. We're using a nonfiction book-launch scenario
as an example because book launches touch upon so many
elements of social media. Not all of these steps are applica-
ble to every situation, but it's useful to see a complete list of
ideas.

Note: Don't try this at the office. This strategy is only
for untrained amateurs. It will make your head explode if

179

you're a trained expert who's accustomed to <u>weeks of strategizing, testing, and consensus-building</u> inside a large agency.

121. Build the Foundation

- Refresh all profiles, avatars, and e-mail signatures and make them match.

- Refresh all bios (*Wikipedia*, website, LinkedIn) and make them match.

- Create author pages on Amazon and Goodreads.

- Activate LinkedIn long-form posting.

- Create a media kit that includes the cover, blurbs, description, bios, and author photos. See the <u>APE kit</u> as an example.

- Create a one-page website for the book. See the <u>APE website</u> as an example.

- Set up Google Alerts to catch book reviews, blog posts, and other mentions of the book or author.

122. Amass Your Digital Assets

- Create a three to four second intro/outro clip with the book cover to use with all other videos.

- Create a thirty-second video about the book. See "How to APE a Book."

- Create two-minute videos about each chapter.

- Write a five-hundred-word blog post about each chapter.

- Write a one-thousand-word LinkedIn long-form post summarizing the book.

- Create graphics with twenty-five to thirty quotes from the book.

- Make a presentation at any TEDx that will have you.

- Provide a copy of the book to anyone who promises to review it.

- Create a SlideShare presentation about the ten key points of the book.

123. Go to Market

- Share at least two curated (as opposed to created) posts per day per platform.

- Share the five-hundred-word posts at the rate of two per week, scheduling them to run out the week before publication day.

- Share the one-thousand-word post on LinkedIn on the day of publication.

- Share the two-minute videos at the rate of two per week, beginning a week after publication.

- Share the graphics with quotes at the rate of two per day, starting on the day of publication.

- Schedule a Twitter chat during the week of publication.

- Schedule a thirty-minute Hangout on Air during the week of publication.

- Schedule a <u>Reddit Ask Me Anything</u> (AMA) during the week of publication.

- Schedule HOAs and podcasts with any bloggers who are interested.

Again, these assets and steps are for a book launch, but they illustrate what you can do with social media for most products and services. This is a long and hard-to-achieve list, but it's not an impossible task. Two people, little ol' Peg and I, do it, so you can too.

Conclusion

Don't cry because it's over, smile because it happened.

DR. SEUSS (OR GABRIEL GARCÍA MÁRQUEZ)

Sometimes it helps to look far outside your field for inspiration. In our case, we found Don Miguel Ruiz, a shamanic healer and spiritualist in the Toltec tradition, and his son Don Jose Ruiz.

In *The Four Agreements: A Practical Guide to Personal Freedom* and *The Fifth Agreement: A Practical Guide to Self-Mastery*, they espouse a simple code for personal conduct:

- Be impeccable with your word.
- Don't take anything personally.
- Don't make assumptions.
- Always do your best.
- Be skeptical but learn to listen.

We could not have come up with better advice for using social media. No matter how social media changes, this code will serve you well.

We've done our best to help you master the art and science of social media, and now we want you to go out and rock the world.

Guy Kawasaki (Guy@canva.com)
and Peg Fitzpatrick (Peg@pegfitzpatrick.com)

List of Apps and Services

The revolution won't be televised . . . but there is an App for that.

GARY WAYNE CLARK,
THE DEVOLUTION CHRONICLES: PASSAGE TO NIBURU

A

<u>Alltop</u>. Aggregation of RSS feeds organized by topic.

B

<u>Buffer</u>. Social-media content-scheduling platform.

C

<u>Camera+</u>. Mobile photo-editing app.
<u>Chrome</u>. Google's Web browser.
<u>ClickToTweet</u>. Service to add clickable links to send tweets.
<u>Color Splash</u>. Mobile photo-editing app.

<u>Creative Commons</u>. Nonprofit organization that enables sharing of creative works; it maintains a front end to search other sharing websites.

D

<u>Diptic</u>. Mobile app for iPhone and iPad to create photo collages.
<u>Do Share</u>. Chrome-based Google+ sharing service for Google+ personal profiles.

F

<u>Facebook</u>. Social-media platform.
<u>Feedly</u>. RSS reader app and service.
<u>Flickr Creative Commons</u>. Flickr collection of Creative Commons photos.
<u>Fotolia</u>. Stock-photography website.
<u>Friends+Me</u>. Service to share Google+ content to other social-media platforms.
<u>Futurity</u>. News-aggregation service for research from top universities.

G

<u>Goodreads</u>. Social network for readers and writers.
<u>Google+</u>. Social-media platform.
<u>Google Scholar</u>. Specialty search engine to find scholarly research.

H

<u>HangoutMagix</u>. Website to create lower-third custom overlays for Google+ Hangouts on Air.
<u>Holy Kaw</u>. Website compilation of human-interest stories.
<u>Hootsuite</u>. Social-media monitoring and scheduling platform.

I

<u>Iconosquare</u>. Instagram desktop viewing site for popular content.
<u>IFTTT (If This Then That)</u>. Utility to connect different websites to do things automatically.

Instagram. Social-media photo-sharing app owned by Facebook.
Instatag. Mobile hashtag app for Instagram.
iStockPhoto. Stock-photography website.

K

Klout. Social-media measurement and content-curation website.

L

LikeAlyzer. Service for Facebook measurement and metrics.
LinkedIn. Professional social-networking platform.

M

MailChimp. Service for e-mail lists.

N

NPR (National Public Radio). Not-for-profit news service.

P

Photo Repost. Mobile app to share other people's Instagram photos.
Pinterest. Social-media platform to share pictures.
Populagram. Service to view popular photos from Instagram on desktop or mobile.
Post Planner. Facebook app for content curation and management.

R

Reddit. User-generated and user-rated Internet news service.
Replies and More. Chrome extension for Google+ that enhances replying to comments.
Repost for Instagram. App for Instagram to reshare photos.

S

SlideShare. Website for sharing presentations.
SmartBrief. News curation and aggregation service.
Snapseed. Mobile photo-editing with Google+ integration.
SocialBro. Twitter monitoring, measurement, and maintenance service.
Sprout Social. Social-media management and measurement service.
Stocksy. Stock-photography website.
Storify. Service to compile stories across social-media platforms.
Stresslimit. Editorial calendar plug-in for WordPress blogs.
StumbleUpon. Website for discovering and rating content.

T

TagsForLikes. Mobile app with hashtags for Instagram.
Tailwind. Pinterest analytics and scheduling website.
Tchat. Twitter chat client.
TED and TEDx. Inspirational speeches presented in eighteen minutes or less.
Triberr. Blogging community that shares members' posts.
Tumblr. Blogging platform.
TweetDeck. App for Twitter.
22Social. Facebook app to run live Google+ Hangouts on Air through Facebook.
Twitter. Social-media platform.
Twubs. Twitter chat client.

W

Wikimedia Commons. Collection of public-domain and freely licensed images, sound clips, and video clips.
Wikiquote. Free online compendium of quotations and their sources.
WiseStamp. Service to create custom e-mail signatures.

Y

YouTube. Video-sharing site.

Index